P9-AGR-208

WITHDRAWN
UTSA LIBRARIES

TWAYNE'S WORLD AUTHORS SERIES
A Survey of the World's Literature

Sylvia E. Bowman, Indiana University
GENERAL EDITOR

SPAIN

Gerald Wade, Vanderbilt University
Janet W. Diáz, University of North Carolina at Chapel Hill
EDITORS

Miguel Mihura

TWAS 436

Miguel Mihura

MIGUEL MIHURA

By DOUGLAS R. McKAY
University of Colorado, Colorado Springs

TWAYNE PUBLISHERS
A DIVISION OF G. K. HALL & CO., BOSTON

Copyright © 1977 by G.K. Hall & Co.
All Rights Reserved
First Printing

Library of Congress Cataloging in Publication Data

McKay, Douglas R
  Miguel Mihura.

  (Twayne's world authors series ; TWAS 436 : Spain)
  Bibliography: p. 145-50.
  Includes index.
  1. Miguel Mihura. 2. Authors, Spanish—20th cen-
  tury—Biography.
PQ6623.I35Z77   868'.6'409   76-54526
ISBN 0-8057-6191-8

LIBRARY
University of Texas
At San Antonio

MANUFACTURED IN THE UNITED STATES OF AMERICA

To the memory of
JOHN A. RAMSEY

Contents

About the Author

Douglas R. McKay is Associate Professor of Spanish and Chairman of the Department of Foreign Language and Literature at the University of Colorado, Colorado Springs. He received his B.A. degree in 1962 from the University of Utah, his M.A. in 1964 from the University of Oregon, and his Ph.D. in 1968 from Michigan State University. He has resided in Uruguay for thirty months, in Spain for one year, and again in Spain, Mexico, and France over several summers.

In addition to *Miguel Mihura*, Professor McKay is the author of two other Twayne critical biographies; *Carlos Arniches* (1972) and *Enrique Jardiel Poncela*. He is editor of *Misterio y pavor: Trece cuentos* (Holt, Rinehart and Winston, 1974). His book reviews and articles have appeared in *Books Abroad, Choice, The Explicator, Hispania, Latin America Literary Review, The Modern Language Journal,* and *Modern Language Notes.* He is currently serving as Review Editor for Spanish publications on the staff of *The Modern Language Journal.*

Preface

Miguel Mihura Santos is one of the most important playwrights in the Spanish contemporary theater. He is the author of twenty-three full-length plays, numerous dramatic sketches, and several imaginative essays about his life and career.

Mihura's reputation as a pioneer in the development of a new articulation of dramatic humor was firmly established between 1936 and 1944. During this period he co-authored two plays of a startling avant-garde flavor and promoted the exciting and bizarre humor of *La Ametralladora* and *La Codorniz,* popular weekly magazines he founded in 1936 and 1941, respectively. Then, in the year 1952, Mihura gained recognition as Spain's leading exponent of humoristic invention with the première of his first and most celebrated production as an independent playwright, *Three Top Hats* (*Tres sombreros de copa*), an audacious comedy he had written as a young man twenty years before.

The staging of *Three Top Hats* climaxed an era of exploration with technique and subject matter. While Mihura's entire theater reflects a spirit of calculated versatility, owing to the author's insistence upon a constant alteration of theme and variety of treatment with each new play, the early dramas differ from his later comedies by dint of their spirit of the absurd couched in unconventional dramatic structure and unfettered by concessions to public demands.

All Mihura's plays embody a distinctly intellectual humor that is at once tender, poetic, enigmatic, and satiric. They reveal a singular attention to subjects of absorbing human concern, to the illusions and the delusions behind authentic aspirations, often viewed with a charitable degree of irony and cynicism. They exemplify, above all, the playwright's exceptional artistry in construction of the kind of dialogue that grows out of genuine personal experience.

The aim of this study is to elucidate the merits and to identify the limitations of Mihura's theatrical writings. To achieve this goal we first examine the facts of his life and career and then define the literary legacy he inherited from those playwrights who played a decisive role in molding a climate propitious for his work. Thereafter our attention shifts to the aesthetic principles and the pre-theatrical writings of Mihura himself. Those chapters devoted to his early dramatic writings, acclaimed as superior literary works compared to the more serene and conservative comedies of his later period, will probe the artistic merits of those memorable plays. Although the quality of his later comedies varies remarkably over the years, ranging from plays of undisputed worth to farces of vapid mediocrity, we have attempted to analyze them all. They are arranged for discussion by genre classification, according to Don Miguel's own suggested categories, namely, the plays of suspense, the comedies of parody and satire, and the richly human character portrayals.

The primary source material utilized for this study is Mihura's published plays. I have been greatly aided by the personal assistance of Sr. Mihura, who kindly provided access to materials otherwise unobtainable, and who granted me several interviews in his Madrid residence during my three visits to the Spanish capital since 1967. In addition, direct communication and later correspondence with several drama critics in Madrid have supplied useful ideas for this study; in this regard I am pleased to single out the names of Juan Emilio Aragonés, José Monleón, and the late Alfredo Marqueríe for special recognition.

I am also grateful to the untiring personnel at Madrid's two major periodical libraries, the Hemeroteca Municipal and the Hemeroteca Nacional. At the former I was privileged to consult the near-complete collection of *La Ametralladora* and all early issues of *La Codorniz,* which have proven to be valuable documents for studying Mihura's nascent dramatic tendencies. The latter institute also provided a representation of contemporary journalistic response to Mihura's plays, a more spontaneous type of critical reaction than that inherent in the more studied critiques of formal articles listed in the Selected Bibliography.

Appreciation is likewise expressed to Ms. Ingeborg Muur of Oslo, Norway, to Sr. Patricio Pérez Cobas of Madrid, and to Professors Marilynn I. Ward, Darlyn D. Davison, and George T. Cabello for enabling me to peruse their investigative efforts on various aspects of Mihurian research. To Professors Janet W. Díaz and Gerald E. Wade I am indebted for the opportunity to undertake this study for Twayne, updating and expanding a research project that had its initial impetus under the highly professional guidance of the late John A. Ramsey of Michigan State University, a man of quiet dignity and sound critical judgment to whose name and memory this book is dedicated.

Finally, I wish to acknowledge the financial assistance of a grant-in-aid from the University of Colorado's Council on Research and Creative Work, as well as the encouragement I have received from Dean A. Paul Ballantyne of the UCCS College of Letters, Arts and Sciences to complete this project.

DOUGLAS R. MCKAY

University of Colorado, Colorado Springs

Chronology

1905   July 21: Miguel Mihura born in Madrid.

1921   Begins seven-year employ under his father at Madrid's Rey Alfonso Theater.

1923   Initiates collaboration as writer and illustrator for various humor magazines.

1925   Death of father, Miguel Mihura Álvarez.

1932   November 10: Completes writing *Three Top Hats* (*Tres sombreros de copa*), his best and most celebrated play.

1934   Writes first movie scripts for Spanish film industry.

1937   January 18: First issue of *La Ametralladora*.

1938   June 26: Final issue of *La Ametralladora*.

1939   November 24: Première of *Long Live the Impossible* (*Viva lo imposible*), written in collaboration with Joaquín Calvo-Sotelo.

1941   June 8: First issue of *La Codorniz*. Mihura directed the journal for thirty-three months.

1943   First publication of *Three Top Hats* (*Tres sombreros de copa*). December 17: Première of *Neither Poor nor Rich, but the Exact Reverse* (*Ni pobre ni rico, sino todo lo contrario*), written in collaboration with Antonio de Lara.

1944   March 26: Final issue (#147) of *La Codorniz* under Mihura's direction.

1946   February 20: Première of *The Case of the Slightly Murdered Woman* (*El caso de la mujer asesinadita*), written in collaboration with Álvaro de Laiglesia.

1948   Publishes *My Memoirs* (*Mis memorias*), a tongue-in-cheek autobiography through the year 1944.

1952   November 24: Première of *Three Top Hats* (*Tres sombreros de copa*).

1953   National Drama Prize conferred for *Three Top Hats*.

1955   April 9: Première of *Sublime Decision* (*Sublime decisión*).

1956   January 11: Première of *My Beloved Juan* (*Mi adorado Juan*). Awarded his second National Drama Prize in recognition for *My Beloved Juan* as best play of 1956.

1959   September 29: Première of *Maribel and the Strange Family* (*Maribel y la extraña familia*). Awarded his third National Drama Prize in recognition for *Maribel* as the best play of 1959.

1963   October 25: Première of *Lovely Dorotea* (*La bella Dorotea*).

1964   September 3: Première of *Ninette and a Gentleman from Murcia* (*Ninette y un señor de Murcia*). Awarded the Calderón de la Barca National Drama Prize for *Ninette*.

1968   September 12: Première of his last play, *Only Love and the Moon Bring Good Fortune* (*Sólo el amor y la luna traen fortuna*).

1972   March: Announces his definitive retirement from active playwriting during conference at Madrid's Círculo de Bellas Artes.

1974   February: Seriously injured in Madrid automobile accident.

1975   July 21: Celebrates his 70th birthday.

CHAPTER 1

Life and Career

MIHURA was twenty-seven years of age when, on the tenth day of November, 1932, he completed writing *Three Top Hats*. While the play was not published until 1943 nor premiered until 1952, the date of its writing represents the point of departure for his subsequent immersion in playwriting following many years of zealous interest in diverse aspects of the theater. The year 1932 is thus a pivotal year toward which the incidents of his youth tended and from which an active involvement in the theater developed.

I *Mihura's Youth*

Two important circumstances in Mihura's boyhood contributed to a propitious climate for the incubation and development of his talents. The first of these was the influence of his father, the actor, author, and theater manager, Miguel Mihura Álvarez. The second was Mihura's personal acquaintance with other theater people, notably several reputable playwrights. When Miguel was born (July 21, 1905), his father, then twenty-eight years old, was a highly esteemed comic actor and an enterprising writer of *zarzuelas* (musical comedies), *sainetes* (one-act farces), and comedies. In the year 1905, for instance, he was playing the lead in *The Evil Shadow* by the Quintero brothers and in *Poor Valbuena* by Carlos Arniches and García Álvarez. At the same time he was writing plays with Ricardo González del Toro, whom Miguel has since praised as his father's "close, loyal, and stupendous collaborator."[1] Inasmuch as his father remained in the acting profession until Miguel was sixteen, we are not surprised to encounter a statement such as this from Mihura's own pen: "At home I heard only talk about the theater, about applause, about song passages, about exits, about comic situations, about successes and failures."[2]

Mihura relates that one of his greatest pleasures was to hide be-

hind an armchair in his father's study, a room teeming with auto-
graphed pictures of famous writers, actors, and actresses. From
there he would listen to his father and González del Toro discuss the
intricacies of stage effects, humor, titles, and denouements, while
they planned a scene for their next play. He recalls the fascination
of frequent visits, beginning at the age of five, to his father's dress-
ing room, and later being privileged to occupy an orchestra seat in
the theater hall, to watch over and over again the same plays.

Mihura learned at an early age what he calls "the terrible jitters
of the theater," that is, onstage timing, backstage control, and the
concern, insecurity, and vanity of performers. Owing primarily to
the immediate example of his father, he acquired above all a great
sympathy for actors and a lasting admiration for the acting profession. This is clearly demonstrated in the intimate and kind regard
he holds for performers as he directs his own plays, and it is likewise borne out in his preference to write a work that will display the
talents of a particular thespian rather than oblige the specifications
of a promoter.

During his years of apprenticeship with his father, observing and
admiring the complexities of theatercraft, Mihura completed his
bachillerato (secondary schooling) at Madrid's Colegio de San
Isidro. He then decided to study music, particularly the piano, imbued with a desire to become a musician. The effort, however,
utterly bored him, and he turned instead to a study of drawing and
of language, principally French. These fields were likewise unful-
filling, though he did profit sufficiently from his French studies to
be able to read the important plays of the modern French theater.
Miguel abandoned his formal education in 1921, the year in which
his father retired as an actor to become theater manager for both
the Teatro Cómico and the Teatro del Rey Alfonso (later renamed
the Arniches) in Madrid. His father employed the young boy, then
sixteen, in the box office of the Rey Alfonso, a position Miguel
relished. It brought him within close proximity of both the stage
performance and the performing artists. He attended rehearsals
daily and never missed a première. Thus acquainted early with the
miseries and jubilations of the acting profession, Mihura learned
firsthand about the theater. "The only thing I didn't learn," he
later wrote, "because I didn't care to, was how to write plays."[3]

Despite his professed disinterest in writing for the theater at this
time, Mihura had already begun to write short articles and stories

for humor magazines. Occasional contributions of sketches and cartoons for the newspapers *La Voz, El Sol,* and *Ya* led to later writing assignments with the pre-war periodicals *Buen Humor, Gutiérrez, Cosquillas,* and *Muchas Gracias,* under the pseudonyms Miguel Santos and El Conde de Pepe. Not infrequently he composed farcical, single-column, one-act sketches in play form, the kind of writing activity in which he later excelled under various pseudonyms for *La Codorniz.*

The year 1921 was decisive in Mihura's formative theater training. At this juncture his interest shifted from actors to authors, a fact coinciding with his father's change in professional status. Paralleling his sensitive awareness of the joys or sorrows of stage artists, he now identified himself on a personal level with the writers who came to his father's theater to read or to rehearse their plays. His father introduced him to such prominent figures as Pedro Muñoz Seca, Carlos Arniches, and Enrique García Álvarez, three of the playwrights who exercised a paramount role in the development of the kind of humor in which Mihura was to distinguish himself a decade later.

Mihura's personal contacts with these dramatists afforded him the experience of open conviviality with dynamic individuals. Their lives and artistic labors contributed to Mihura's choice of career; they facilitated his insight into the formulation of theater from its creation to its realization. While not prompted to write a play at this time, Mihura acquired an aesthetic stimulation and a practical understanding of dramaturgy through his boyhood acquaintance with established playwrights. From his actor and actress friends he learned the great importance of a triumph or a failure. From his father Mihura learned the complexities and compensations of stagecraft. Joaquín Aguirre Bellver unerringly states that "Mihura's theater is, first of all, an unbridled youthful vocation, born of the interrelationship with his father and the interrelationship with his surroundings."[4]

II *Early Playwriting and Film Work*

A few years after the death of his father in 1925, an event occurred which had a direct bearing on the writing of *Three Top Hats (Tres sombreros de copa).* The full particulars of this episode, together with an account of the problems involved in the production of his best play, are colorfully chronicled in the prologue to the 1943 edition of *Three Top Hats*. According to Mihura's own report, he once toured the Spanish provinces for twenty days as director of a rather strange troupe of actors. The troupe consisted of six blonde Viennese dancers, a French dancing instructor, a black dancer from Canada, another black dancer from Cuba, and a fat German snake charmer accompanied by his two snakes. The play *Three Top Hats* clearly had its inception in this tour.[5] The fact that the black Buby Barton, the vivacious dancers, their suitors, and the other extraordinary characters who invade Dionisio's hotel room were directly inspired from this incident of real life, indicates Mihura's penchant for converting some unexpected and seemingly unbelievable details from actual circumstances into an equally incongruous but meaningful dramatic context.

A further example of this tendency can be noted in the chain of events that gave rise to *Peaches and Syrup* (*Melocotón en almíbar*)[6] Early in 1958 Mihura attended the American movie "Rififí" in San Sebastián. He then returned to his hotel, bothered by a headcold, and sat in the lobby to order a cognac. At that moment a group of nuns arriving from Lourdes pulled up in a car, and one of them sat down near Mihura to write a postcard. Suddenly the subject matter for a new play burst upon him. The strange admixture of gangsters from "Rififí", a bad cold, and a returning expedition of nuns suggested to Mihura's imagination all the amusing contrasts and possibilities we find realized in his comedy, *Peaches and Syrup*.[7] In fact, Mihura's personal experiences have prevailed upon all his works, so that his plays are never the result of a total imaginative effort. "I find it easy to write about women and amorous adventures, especially those I've lived," he once remarked.[8] On another occasion he confessed that "all of my plays are inspired in something real, in some small personal observation."[9]

Following his twenty-day excursion, Mihura returned to Madrid to collaborate intensely on newspaper articles and to write dialogues for three movie scripts. He was not long in discovering the financial advantages of writing scripts and adapting dialogues for the Spanish film industry. Between the years 1934 and 1952 he worked as dubber and dialoguist on twenty-five motion pictures.[10] His plays *My Beloved Juan* (*Mi adorado Juan*) and *A No-Account Woman* (*Una mujer cualquiera*) were first written as movie scripts (both in 1949), then later adapted for the legitimate stage.[11]

Mihura's film activity became more and more intensified over these eighteen years because of his progressive disillusionment with the theater, which prior to the popular triumph of *Three Top Hats* had given him meager economic returns. *The Case of the Slightly Murdered Woman* (*El caso de la mujer asesinadita*) for instance, drew a profit of only twelve thousand pesetas, or two hundred dollars.[12]

Mihura was comfortable as a film dubber and script writer, preferring the almost anonymous labor, free from publicity, which this vocation allowed him. He habitually shunned public notoriety during his movie career period but was instantly catapulted into national and international prominence with the stage success of *Three Top Hats,* an event which determined once and for all the course and future career to which he would devote the rest of his life. The choice was a logical outgrowth of his upbringing and professional connections. A complex of numerous activities had molded and motivated the poet within him to respond in proportion to the opportunities he seized in his zealous ambition to succeed, "working as little as possible and earning as much money" as was within his power.[13]

III *Aesthetic Principles*

It is important that we define some of Mihura's aesthetic principles to better appreciate certain aspects peculiar to his comedies. For instance, he has consistently maintained, since the production of *Three Top Hats,* that he writes each play geared to please the public's taste and designed to suit the acting talents of a given performer.[14] Knowing this fact readily explains his adoption of conservative precepts and answers as well the strength of his leading characters.

Mihura wrote his first four plays with a carefree disregard for public taste, but after 1952 he adopted a different attitude. He thereafter made willing concessions to his audience, accommodating theme and treatment for easy digestion. This posture has provoked adverse criticism from those who would have Mihura remain in the absurdist tradition of his earlier productions. Pérez Minik, for example, has charged Mihura with having deliberately prostituted dramatic art by a regression to formulas of reactionary theater.[15] Evaristo Acevedo likewise censures Mihura's change in attitude toward his art, objecting to what he considers to be the author's aesthetic desertion from pure humor into common comedy.[16] These statements show that Mihura's position does not enjoy a unanimous endorsement from the critics. Yet despite some objections to his work, the author has insisted upon writing only "to please the public's desires and to try to promote entertainment, as long as it is done with dignity and decency."[17] Perhaps his most incisive remark in defense of this attitude is the following statement he made in 1957 for an article about himself, published in the theatrical magazine, *Primer Acto:* "I believe that the theater is a spectacle for the majority and therefore, one way or another, one must touch the mentality of all theatergoers. . . . I write the way I do because I am that way and I think that way. And I cannot write in any other form."[18]

The creditable aspect of his position, aside from arguing for the excellent literary quality of some of Mihura's works, is his conscious effort to vary the technique and treatment of each play. The idea of prescribing his style to mechanized guidelines terrifies him; his greatest desire is to avoid being categorized as a functionary of the theater: "I would prefer to have no style at all, and to write each play different from the others."[19]

During his nearly thirty years of playwriting, Mihura premiered his comedies infrequently, though he spent no more than two to three months writing them. His premières may best be described as erratic and unpredictable. Several seasons would go by without his name appearing on the billboards, then, during one year, he might feature three plays simultaneously. He generally shunned a regular routine of productivity, for, as he admitted to Ángel Laborda, a too frequent appearance invites "too much unpleasantness, many disillusions, and multiple disenchantments."[20] This was the case with his unusually prolific staging of three productions during the 1964–65 season, which left him a spent man, embittered over theatercraft, and eager for a speedy retirement.[21] Mihura found that for several years his ideal program was to begin writing a play in May, to rehearse the first act in June, and to conclude the comedy by mid-summer, in time to have it premiered by September. He believed it essential that he be the only person responsible for its production; he therefore directed all of his own plays: "There must be no interferences. If I am to go on staging plays, I will personally direct my works."[22]

IV *Personal Life-Style*

Miguel Mihura has delighted in cultivating the image of a literary vagrant. He still boasts of being perennially lazy, obliged to regulate his life from one siesta to the next.[23] During an occasional burst of energy, often occurring between five and eight in the evening, he would write, correct, and type his plays in the comfort of his book-lined study. This labor, Mihura says, was often accompanied by a great yearning to go back to bed. "I would be happy if I could spend my entire life lying down and reading in bed," he once declared.[24] Sheer boredom produced the three plays he feverishly premiered during the atypical 1964–65 season.

Mihura recalls with pleasure the days when with a group of friends, he would write his plays at *tertulias,* but he admits that his present-day habits require a torturous labor of solitude. He attempts to enliven the painful sessions of creativity by writing with multiple colors on gigantic blocks of heavy folio paper that he buys in Paris.

Don Miguel is a confirmed bachelor. Until 1970 he enjoyed a good deal of female company. For approximately five years he was involved with a Norwegian student, a relatively young girl who had come to Madrid to write her doctoral thesis on Mihura and remained as his mistress. Mihura admits that only once since that time did he come "dangerously close" to considering marriage. He now lives a quiet, sedate life, preferring ingrained habits over a busy social climate that would disturb his rest. In recent years Mihura has divided his time between his Madrid home at number 97 General Pardiñas and a vacation residence at Paseo Iribarren, 6, in Fuenterrabia. He injured both legs in an automobile collision in February of 1974, resulting in a painful six-month convalescence in his Madrid residence. Since then he has experienced considerable discomfort from arthrosis of the knee joints and finds it increasingly difficult to walk without severe pain.

He has written nothing for the stage since 1968 and plans to do little more beyond writing an introduction for a forthcoming Aguilar edition of his complete works and perhaps revising the still unpublished play, *Canasta (La canasta)*. He broods pessimistically about "the wretched state of the world," confessing to a world-weary sadness and boredom, a total dislike for the society in which he lives, a disdain toward and ignorance about the contemporary theater, and a preference for living out his life in solitude. Despite his cynicism, Miguel Mihura is an affable and good-tempered man; he is enormously pleased to have utilized his few waking hours each day to generate through drama some laughter and smiles of human enjoyment.

CHAPTER 2

Twentieth-Century Precursors

MIGUEL Mihura's literary line of descent passes varyingly through Carlos Arniches (1866–1943), Enrique García Álvarez (1873–1931), Pedro Muñoz Seca (1881–1936), and Enrique Jardiel Poncela (1901–52). These writers are frequently mentioned as the principal dramatists in the theater of absurd humor of twentieth-century Spain.[1] Their legacy to Mihura represents more an aesthetic conditioning than a functional inventory of technical resources. For a period of almost fifty years they excited a new artistic response to the validity of humor in the legitimate theater; they seasoned both playgoer and critic for the digestion of novelty within the framework of a traditional form.

These playwrights, however, do not represent a clearly defined movement of literary intention. Despite their mutual collaborations, they evince no apparent disposition to formulate a school. Collectively they generate a climate conducive to the formation of Miguel Mihura's theater; individually no single writer mentioned above qualifies as a consummate precursor of the latter's style and technique. Indeed, Mihura's early plays, while similar in scope to the humoristic innovations of his predecessors, are uniquely original. They represent an all-too-radical departure from the recognized theater forms of his day and thus cannot be considered the logical outgrowth of a unified, linear evolvement.

Because of their relevance to Mihura's early life, the respective theatrical legacies of the above-named playwrights warrant a passing consideration. While they may not constitute a measured or concerted effort to establish a new current of dramatic humor by conscious design, there is evidence to support the idea that without their pioneering, Mihura's theater would have been impossible.

I *Carlos Arniches*

When Mihura was still a young boy, not over eleven years of age, yet thoroughly exposed even then to the life and concerns of the theater, Carlos Arniches y Barrera was already in his fiftieth year, in the prime of his creative work. Arniches, the indisputable master of the contemporary *sainete,* had begun to cultivate a startling new genre in his repertory of dramatic forms, the *tragedia grotesca* (grotesque tragedy).[2] Mihura admired this latter phase over and above Arniches' previous productions, particularly its stress on the subjective involvement of the protagonist in a struggle for positive heroism. Mihura recalls having witnessed the dreadful opening-night fear of Arniches who, despite having premiered well over one hundred works and being the most acclaimed author of the time, would come down to the box office during a première and remain at Mihura's side, "pale, silent, distraught, awaiting the public's verdict."[3]

In his mature years, Arniches developed a more complete and delicate sense of construction in his plays, transforming and transfiguring the popular themes of the *sainete* into what Pedro Salinas terms "a game of external comicity and profound gravity."[4] Salinas correctly views the grotesque tragedy as a fundamentally serious form of drama. It resembles the serious intentions of Mihura's theater in its emphasis on the value of the human personality, stressing the validity of constant, guileless ties with one's fellow beings. Like Mihura's theater, it is also tinged with occasional concessions to obtain comic effects; yet these are governed by a natural spontaneity that furnishes us with the "creation of authentic humor beneath the trappings of a *comedietta.*"[5] This is to say that in their respective theaters we are not exposed to artificial and shallow comedy; their humor is controlled by an underlying literary substance that avoids falsification or pure frivolity for its own sake. The authors disengage themselves from their respective characters and from the plot line to permit their creations a clear autonomy of expression.

The moral and human dimension that characterizes the grotesque tragedy is sustained by yet another element common to Mihura's early productions. This is the ever-increasing importance assigned to a language that is original, expressive, and often nonsensical, intentionally sprinkled with word plays and figures of speech, especially hyperbole. It is this aspect which prompted one critic to judge the grotesque tragedy as an authentic expression of the modern world and of human life, out of which the comic types, absurd actions, and verbal dislocations of Muñoz Seca's theater were to evolve.[6]

The principal merit attributed to Arniches is the same virtue that Mihura values the most in his writings — the ability to manipulate dialogue to fit a particular situation. Arniches' theater is solidly and fundamentally one of language. "The power of the spoken word" is its cornerstone, states Marquerie, and "what the characters say is far more vital than what they do."[7] The same may be said for Mihura's comedies. As a youngster, Mihura was forcibly impressed by this feature in the aging playwright's theater; indeed, Arniches' comically deformed words made an impact on Mihura's entire generation. The incredibly funny *disparates* (absurdities) and the ingenious but improvident reasonings of his dialogues were Carlos Arniches' foremost contributions to the present-day theater. In the old master's work, Mihura found a superlative example of "the enormous theatrical efficacy of dialogue."[8]

II   *Enrique García Álvarez*

García Álvarez also occupies a unique position in the development of dramatic humor before Mihura. His name is usually paired with one of several other playwrights, for he was an indefatigable collaborator who rarely produced plays on his own.[9] He is also the acknowledged creator of a new genre in the Spanish theater, a comic prescription that bears the name *astracán,* a farcical composition in which dialogue is central to the comic situation and verisimilitude is deliberately reduced.[10]

Among all of his elderly dramatist acquaintances, Mihura's most cherished friend was García Álvarez who at the age of fifty was still responding to the changing demands of theater managers and the public. Mihura valued the importance of this extraordinary personality to such an extent as to assign to him a kind of patriarchal role in the development of his own and other's dramatic efforts. In 1943 he wrote of García Álvarez as "the author whom I have most admired in my youth, the most nonsensical, the least bourgeois, perhaps the master of those of us who afterwards began to cultivate a theater of the absurd."[11]

García Álvarez inaugurated an entirely new approach, and his *astracán* formulas undoubtedly had a significant influence on Mihura's quasi-dramatic writings for the magazines *Gutiérrez, Buen Humor, La Ametralladora,* and *La Codorniz,* as well as on his early plays, although to date no study on the subject has emerged. It may be seen at some future time that Mihura's avant-garde theater represents a refinement and consummation of the *astracán* technique. But García Álvarez's primary contribution to the theater of his day lies not alone in his "comic playlets sustained by the strength of puns," which González Ruiz deprecates;[12] his importance must also be assessed by virtue of the weight and value he gives to dialogue as the dominant feature of dramatic humor, the same formula which Arniches recognized and utilized for his major successes, which Muñoz Seca employed in a multitude of plays, and which Jardiel Poncela enhanced by adding greater rapidity of speech to fast-moving comic situations. These precedents Mihura polished and perfected, bringing into focus the tenderness, vigor, and drama of the human personality.

García Álvarez's work was concluded in 1931, thus ending what Mihura has ironically called "the most extraordinary case of vagrancy in the modern theater," referring to the playwright's frequently changing collaborations and boundless energy.[13] His role in the development of the contemporary theater of humor remains grossly underrated and merits a serious revaluation.

III   *Pedro Muñoz Seca*

While García Álvarez is the recognized initiator of the *astracán,* its chief architect and producer is Pedro Muñoz Seca. The two men co-authored eight plays between 1914 and 1916, and thereafter Muñoz Seca continued to write innumerable plays on his own in the same *astracán* tradition.[14] Under his prolific authorship the *astracán* develops from a moderate exuberance in dialogue into the most lavish exhibition of vocalized nonsense to be witnessed on the Spanish stage. The drama critic González Ruiz terms the quarter-century of the *astracán's* currency a time of "frenzied exaggeration and absurdity."[15] It was during this period that Muñoz Seca reigned supreme as its foremost advocate, producing with notable technical skill what Valbuena Prat labels "a theater of absolute absurdity, of total jest."[16]

Except for enlarging upon the *astracán,* restating its design and composition with increased comic effect, Muñoz Seca adds no new dimensions to the original concept. Its basic formula of dislocated speech and comic jests, its illogical characterizations and implausible happenings, he fully exploits without noticeable deviation or mutation until late in his career. He perpetuates an established trend, merely intensifying the impact of its humor with a stress on colloquial wit and an occasional gibe or sneer, described by one of his admirers as being "somewhat sarcastic, crackling, explosive, rapid, and unexpected."[17] These characteristics heighten the comedy of his plays and distinguish his theater from the more subdued absurdist humor detectable in Arniches and García Álvarez.

In further contrast to the plays of García Álvarez, we find in the theater of Muñoz Seca an increased concentration on exaggerated situations and a deliberate effort to caricature the society and events of his own day. This is particularly true in the final phase of his writing career, when he employs the *astracán* as a fierce political weapon, its jokes and barbs intended to parody, satirize, and burlesque the contemporary scene. Yet even in his combative and satirical period, Muñoz Seca attempts no radical departure from the basic resources and devices of the *astracán* which he inherited from his close friend and fellow collaborator. His farce, unlike that of García Álvarez, is incisive and dominantly germane to current problems, but by no means acrimonious or pessimistic. It is more likely that the strong tinge of cynicism underlying Mihura's early theater is an outgrowth of Jardiel's drama rather than a reflection of Muñoz Seca's lightly corrosive but basically optimistic satire.

Muñoz Seca's importance with regard to later developments in the theater also lies in the attention he devotes to dialogue as the primary vehicle for humor, a dialogue independent of the stylized inventions of Arniches, and free from the *costumbrista* leanings of García Álvarez. It is this special sense of dialogue, this insistence on the validity of the comic utterance that, when later tempered and shorn of its rough and often unkind properties, becomes the hallmark of Miguel Mihura's theater.

Muñoz Seca generated plays as rapidly as he appropriated new notions. To a large extent, his success and reputation as the leading promoter of the *astracán* was based on his amazingly rich productivity. His name was constantly before the public. At the age of forty he was premiering an average of ten plays a year. Mihura was then fifteen years old and informs us that he never missed a première of this renowned humorist.[18] Mihura remembers Muñoz Seca as a most ingenious, cordial, and optimistic gentleman, whose talents and inventiveness left the young boy in constant wonder. During the years that Miguel was engaged in the business end of theater life (1921–1928), attending with interest all current productions in Madrid, Muñoz Seca premiered fifty-five plays in the Spanish capital.[19] This fact alone indicates the tremendous amount of exposure young Mihura had to the theater of that venerated playwright whose twenty-nine-year career produced over 170 plays.

Those who assess the importance of twentieth-century Spanish drama are seemingly divided in their evaluation of Muñoz Seca. The widest disagreement concerning his literary merit exists between the stated opinions of literary artists, who value his legacy of unrestrained humor and theatrical inventiveness over his sociopolitical posture, and those of the drama critics, who accuse him of removing the *astracán* from the domain of literature and prostituting its inherently atemporal formulas by confinement within the arena of politics and social criticism.

Azorín, for example, is one of Muñoz Seca's most ardent defenders. He lauds the rigorous construction of his plays and suggests that had he been a Frenchman his statue would have been crowned with laurel and placed on the Elysian Fields, but as a Spaniard he was lucky to have had a street named after him.[20] Jardiel Poncela also praises the definitive literary accomplishments of the playwright, ranking him second only to García Álvarez as the most important dramatic writer of his time.[21] Alfonso Paso pays him high tribute in a serious essay discussing his artistic skills.[22] Mihura likewise affirms a lifelong admiration for the energy, optimism, creativity, and imagination of Muñoz Seca; indeed, Mihura relates that as a young man he often defended the older playwright's reputation, "at the top of his voice in the theater lobbies when some stupid and indiscreet old man tried to attack him."[23]

As for the attacks Mihura speaks of, they too have been legion, not only from "stupid and indiscreet old men," but also from responsible critics and writers of sound judgment. A favorable biography, published as early as 1939, did little to invalidate Muñoz Seca's growing disrepute as a writer of merely marginal literary significance.[24] Such is the position of Gonzalo Torrente Ballester, who finds his theater confused and contradictory, "lacking great literary importance, but of enormous social importance."[25] In an earlier article Torrente discredits the *astracán* altogether as a literary genre, pointing to the negative and destructive elements of its development in the later plays of Muñoz Seca.[26] Juan Chabás is explicitly condemnatory in his consideration of the *astracán,* stating that "the genre should be expelled from ... the history of the theater."[27] This negative sentiment is echoed in the writings of several other major critics and literary historians, most of whom base their unfavorable comments upon the dramatist's plays after 1930.[28] Yet virtually all of the critics — detractors as well as apologists — are in unanimous accord as to the historical importance of the comic factor in his theater. His innovative sallies represent "the germ of a later theater."[29] In a general sense, their revolutionary flavor inaugurates a distinctive phase of the theater of the absurd in Spanish literature, insofar as language is concerned. The critic Francisco García Pavón has Muñoz Seca's *astracán* in mind when he writes that "the theater of humor entails the only authentic vanguard of Spanish dramatic art."[30]

Thus the theater of Muñoz Seca represents an essential link in the chain of dramatic satire, connecting a pre-war theater of farcical humor, designed largely to amuse and to entertain, with post-war social satire of a somewhat more corrosive and serious intent. Miguel Mihura inherits the proven formula, verified in his best plays, that dialogue constitutes the most authentic medium for conveying a humor that, when devoid of topical imprecations, is pregnant with meaning and literary value. Muñoz Seca's tendency to satirize the current scene is sparingly reflected in Mihura's theater, but while Muñoz disowns his epoch with obvious exasperation, Mihura, as we shall see, accepts his world as he finds it, adding a new dimension of human compassion and poetic tenderness to soften the more negative features.

IV *Enrique Jardiel Poncela*

Of the four dramatists under discussion, Jardiel Poncela is Mihura's most immediate contemporary. Only four years separate their respective ages, Jardiel being the elder. Yet his first major success, *A Sleepless Spring Night* (1927), precedes Mihura's initial production by a full twelve years, and Jardiel had already staged eleven unsuccessful plays before that date. The beginning of his theater corresponds chronologically to the advent of Muñoz Seca's sociopolitical satires; it represents, in fact, a combative effort opposing "the *astracán* of vulgar extraction," which Pérez Minik calls "coarse, crowd-pleasing formulas" of Muñoz Seca.[31] It is superfluous to recount Jardiel's theatrical innovations. Several biographies and monographs have treated the subject well since the year 1945, providing evidence that a large segment of critical opinion declares for Jardiel's decisive influence on the Spanish comic theater.[32] Uppermost for our present concern, however, is Jardiel's direct connection with Mihura and the extent to which the younger playwright was affected by his predecessor's "deliberately off-center and caricatural theater."[33]

During the years 1927–1934 Jardiel and Mihura collaborated frequently on articles for the magazines *Buen Humor* and *Gutiérrez*. Together they espoused an aesthetic posture shared by Antonio de Lara, Edgar Neville, and José López Rubio, among others — that is, a desire to renew and rejuvenate Spanish comedy. Their individual efforts fomented a startling new direction in humor, where parody, caricature, irony, and satire were combined in a struggle against the banality and dullness of everyday communication. When Jardiel detached himself from journalistic endeavors to further this trend in the theater, his independent inventiveness tended toward progressive extravagance of comic situation, a withdrawal from explicable plot lines, and a penchant for elaborating upon abstraction and incongruency, resulting in perpetuation of the absurdist spirit in Spanish drama, a movement tagged by Marquerie as *el Jardielismo* in contemporary literature.[34]

Mihura, on the other hand, inclined toward a more natural, simple, and humanized world, never losing sight of the relevance for sound character portrayal of the circumstances of a recognizable milieu. Mihura's theater would reflect greater judgment and penetration into the profundities of human nature, while Jardiel's plays displayed uninhibited farce where a highly histrionic and artificial comedy was maintained by means of visual effects, slapstick, and rapidity of stage action.

Both Jardiel and Mihura have enough in common, however, to be classified as humorists of the same basic stock. An identical striving to avoid worn and tired forms in comedy is apparent in each writer. The same search for the unusual and the imaginative characterizes their respective theaters. They coincide in a flight from verisimilitude as an expressed scorn for realistic comedy.

They share equally the spirit of the early *astracán* with its absurdist humor and its fondness for parody and punning. Their similarities in this regard are so close, in fact, that Jardiel once angrily accused Mihura of plagiarism, referring to some of the latter's writings for *La Codorniz*. Alfredo Marquerie invalidates this charge by stating that Jardiel was hounded by jealousy; that upon learning of Mihura's increasing popularity, Jardiel foresaw the rank Mihura was to attain in the annals of the modern Spanish drama. Jardiel was piqued, reports Marquerie, to have discovered an able competitor rather than a mere disciple, and thus he reverted to sarcasm and disdain.[35] The feud was shortlived, and Mihura speaks today with high regard of Jardiel, whose theater, he claims, "contributed to prepare theatergoers for our way of understanding humor."[36] Mihura, incidentally, now views his own theater as a totally distinct phenomenon from Jardiel's: "What I write is an intimate and personal theater. Jardiel's is one of involved plots. But what we both share in common is belonging to the same generation."[37]

Jardiel's revitalizing energy gave rise to a new respect for the whole area of popular comedy in Spain. Professor Juan R. Castellano remarked that of all Spanish playwrights who have written since this man, only Antonio de Lara and Mihura have achieved greater success in the Jardielesque tradition; the latter represent, through their play *Neither Poor Nor Rich, but the Exact Reverse* (*Ni pobre ni rico, sino todo lo contrario*), the consummation of an epoch. "Jardielesque humor," Dr. Castellano wrote, "marks the transition between the parody of Muñoz Seca and the post-war theater of humor."[38]

Jardiel transmitted to Mihura an example of skilled technical versatility. He illustrated the performability of freedom within the restrictive structure of a play. He showed how to use the popularly accepted detective or mystery play, a comedy of intrigue and entanglement that Mihura, among others, has since essayed with great success. He bequeathed as well an object lesson in the titles of his plays, which feature bizarre and unusual wording, geared to attract, shock, or startle the playgoer. Above all, Jardiel preserved for Mihura's improved handling the salient trait his forerunners had fostered: the form of comedy wherein dialogue carries a considerable burden of meaning and takes precedence over stage action; where the language per se approximates the formulas of the theater of the absurd. Mihura was to become the central and consummate artist of his generation in this linguistic emphasis, though clearly his way had been prepared by the verve, the exuberance, the inventive word play, and the hyperbolic playfulness with language that characterized the comic dialogues of Jardiel.

We have attempted to underscore the significance of influence in Miguel Mihura's theater, citing some general affinities he shares in common with his most distinguished precursors. The nature of this study limits our consideration to the above-named writers alone. A complete list of those responsible for the formulation of a new framework of theatrical aesthetics in the first half of the twentieth century would also include such names as Joaquín Calvo-Sotelo, Alejandro Casona, Antonio de Lara, Álvaro de Laiglesia, José López Rubio, Edgar Neville, José María Pemán, Víctor Ruiz Iriarte, and Alfonso Paso, not to mention the vital sway and motivation exerted upon this generation by the pens of Ramón del Valle-Inclán and Ramón Gómez de la Serna, whose respective connections with the absurdist trend in Spanish drama is fundamental but as yet only superficially studied.

Mihura, then, is a member of a unique generation of comic playwrights, all responding to the incitement and inspiration of a common ambiance, yet disengaged from promoting a conscious, collective effort which might constitute a literary school. The problem in ascribing direct influences on Mihura is primarily speculative; indeed, Mihura himself is disinclined to admit having sought ideas or inspiration from any single forerunner, notwithstanding the exemplary patterns from which he could well have molded his theater.[39] Mihura prefers to be considered among those who partook of a similar vocation, who shared a strong bond of conviviality, and who individually fostered a new and provocative type of humor, owing to the stimulus of a given historical moment. The famous Italian humorist Pitigrilli, whose *Dialogued Tales* have been compared to Mihura's bizarre playlets and sketches written for *La Codorniz,* has taken a similar position with respect to the idea of a coincidental rapport among members of the same generation. In a letter directed to Mihura from Paris, dated May 19, 1965, Pitigrilli states: "You and I were in the air. It is a coincidence of time, of evolution."[40]

CHAPTER 3

La Codorniz

TWO important journalistic activities conducive to Mihura's success in playwriting were his founding of *La Ametralladora* (1936–1939) and his directorship of *La Codorniz* (1941–1944). In the former publication Mihura shared the editor's task with Edgar Neville and Antonio de Lara, two playwrights who had begun writing independently "an abstract and outlandish humor"[1] as early as 1928. *La Ametralladora* was a wartime miscellany of surface humor taken mainly from borrowed sources, principally Italian, and designed to entertain Nationalist trench soldiers.[2] It brought in an enormous revenue — some three million pesetas.[3]

With the exception of its last page, the early issues of *La Ametralladora* cultivated a frivolous, slapstick vein of humor specifically designed "to encourage the infantry to fight with a happy spirit and a determined heart."[4] The final page, however, carried the ominous caption "Completely Serious." It generally displayed photographs of mutilated compatriots and propagandistic messages.

Mihura relocated the main office and press for *La Ametralladora* several different times as combat pressures shifted. The first fifteen issues were published in Salamanca; but on May 2, 1937 the magazine moved to Valladolid. It returned to Salamanca the following July and was disseminated weekly to nearly 100,000 combatants. On October 3 of that year it was again transplanted, this time to Franco's northern stronghold, Bilbao, where it remained until its final issue in June of 1938. By this time the weekly publication was fervently pro-Franco and zealously patriotic.[5]

Mihura's contributions to *La Ametralladora* consisted largely of recast articles, anecdotes, quips, and cartoons previously published in *Gutiérrez* and other slick magazines.[6] Of interest to students of his theater are the occasional dialogue sketches appearing on the magazine's enormous pages; they contain the kind of absurd humor characteristic of his first published plays. Sometimes Mihura writes these playlets under a pseudonym, but more often he leaves them unsigned.[7] Several reappear later in *La Codorniz* under a new title and a slightly revamped content. Thus Mihura's short-lived wartime periodical represents a transitional conveyance for many of his notions on comedy: they began in *Gutiérrez,* were revised for *La Ametralladora,* and given their definitive form in *La Codorniz.*

Mihura founded the engaging weekly magazine of twenty-four pages, *La Codorniz,* in 1941,[8] directed it until 1944, then relinquished his post to Alvaro de Laiglesia, having become "weary of so much foolishness."[9] The enterprise proved especially lucrative and provided Mihura with abundant opportunities to experiment further with his bizarre playlets.

The early issues of *La Codorniz* have a special fascination by virtue of the particular writers who contributed zany material to its pages. Mihura's collaborators on the original editorial staff included Wenceslao Fernández Flórez, Antonio de Lara, Enrique Jardiel Poncela, Alfredo Marquerie, Joaquín Calvo-Sotelo, Manuel Halcón, Tomás Borrás, Manuel Aznar, and José López Rubio. Edgar Neville, who had labored with Mihura on *La Ametralladora,* joined *La Codorniz'* staff by the seventh issue (July 20, 1941), and his other co-worker from the wartime periodical, Álvaro de Laiglesia, *La Codorniz'* second manager, became an associate early in 1943. After one year of publication under Mihura, *La Codorniz* was featuring one-act plays by the Italian humorists Carlos Manzoni and Victorio Metz, along with occasional novelettes by the controversial Spanish playwright Jardiel Poncela.[10] By the end of its second year, during the same period in which Mihura and Tono (de Lara) were staging *Neither Poor Nor Rich, but the Exact Reverse,* the incomparable humorist Ramón Gómez de la Serna also was contributing articles, quips, and his inimitable *greguerías* to the magazine.[11]

Mihura, as director, frequently signed his writings with the pseudonym El Conde de Pepe. He added jokes, short stories, imaginary interviews, nonsensical letters, and a miscellany of dialogues and fillers to every issue. The last to carry his name as editor was issue number 147, dated March 26, 1944. *La Codorniz* acquired a disputed social importance under Mihura's direction.

The promoter of one rival publication, Cristino Soravilla of *Cú-Cú,* circulated the thesis that its humor was of Italian origin, that Mihura's writings were nothing more than a plagiarized version of the abstract nonsense appearing in *Bertoldo,* the magazine admired and subsidized by Mussolini's government. This accusation gave rise to a lengthy polemic that splashed over into the newsprint of Madrid's *El Español* and generated several interesting discussions pertaining to the meaning and uniqueness of Spanish humor.[12] Although Mihura grew indignant and was visibly disgusted by the controversy, he turned it to his own advantage by promoting widespread sales for *La Codorniz* and by launching his own brand of *Codorniz* humor on the legitimate stage. The humorist Mingote attributes to Mihura's directorship of *La Codorniz* and his subsequent playwriting the origin of "an authentic boom of humor" produced in Spain during the first half of the 1940's.[13]

With apparent but innocuous cynicism, *La Codorniz* became, in the words of Pedro Laín Entralgo, "the sign and mirror of a generation."[14] It ignored conventional lines of humor to foster an atemporal and abstract satire destined, according to López Rubio, one of its regular contributors, to destroy "that which is flimsy, decrepit, dusty, and corrupt."[15] This destructive intention, however, was directed solely at lampooning trite and stale commonplaces in human discourse, attitudes, and reactions. It was definitely not a socially combative or caustic, vituperative type of humor. Spain was convalescing from a grievous civil war, and Mihura's journal would have gained nothing by openly exploiting delicate moral or political issues.[16] Its hallmark was a distancing from reality, an escapist course which deliberately avoided the painful topics of daily living, yet satirized the banal clichés of everyday speech. Mihura concentrated on nineteenth-century settings and an occasional satire of the 1920's but couched his absurdist treatment of those periods in a hazy atemporality that could easily transfer his dialogues to our own day as well as to the time in which they were written.

The following complete playlet is a typical example of Mihura's style in *La Codorniz,* a highly abstract, intellectual humor that achieves its sustained tone of incongruity by presenting a series of unexpected replies in place of the anticipated platitudes of everyday conversation. It is particularly interesting to note that the date of

this original sketch (1942) anticipates by several years the French
theater of the absurd:

She: You dance very well. Is your name by chance Vincent?
He: Not I. And yours?
She: Mine neither.
He: What a coincidence! Two human beings get together and neither one
       is named Vincent!
She: That certainly is a coincidence.
He: This is the first time that's happened to me. But then, since I've only
       lived for four days....
She: You haven't lived for more than four days?
He: Possibly. Sometimes, five.
She: Then you have never known what a Sunday is?
He: Yes, I know what it is, but I've never seen one. Is it very large?
She: A lot like a Monday, but taller.
He: Come now, Vincent!
She: But why Vincent?
He: Didn't you tell me your name is Vincent?
She: Yes, but very little.
He: When you care to, let's quit dancing because the music stopped over
       a week ago.[17]

Many readers were understandably outraged by this nonsense.
Some charged Mihura for spreading an unhealthy spirit of icono-
clasm throughout Spanish society, though Mihura insisted that the
only true debunking he intended was restricted to an exploitation of
the tiresome clichés of common discourse. Nonetheless, Mihura's
articles were assailed by a legion of impassioned detractors who
harassed him constantly. He finally became so exasperated as to
resign in disgust, commenting that "the fighting, the controversy,
and the notoriety are inconsistent with my gentle, retiring, and
timid nature."[18]

Throughout the thirty-three months of Mihura's directorship
and writing for *La Codorniz,* one finds that his brand of humor
clearly anticipates the shift in style and taste that ultimately led to
the recognition of a new aesthetic toward language in Western
European literature. As early as 1928 Edgar Neville, Tono, and
Mihura were each writing a humor of incongruity that employed inverted platitudes, repetitions, irony, illogical statements, and
absurd monologues to tease the reader with a flippant raillery
against timeworn expressions. The humorists popularized a new

kind of dialogue in Spain, a repartee bereft of internal logic and calculated to elicit laughter by the intentional deformation of the trite, mechanical formulas of everyday speech.

Mihura and Tono carried this campaign into their later film work. Their art at dubbing evoked high praise because they successfully converted colorless dialogue into a hilarious parody of itself. One mediocre German film was hailed "a work of first order" following Mihura and Tono's work at dubbing: "They gave it an absurd dialogue, delightful for its incongruities, ... of an inventive and satiric spirit."[19] Wherever they applied it, the bizarre language they utilized was labeled *humor codornicesco*. Working sometimes with Tono, other times with Neville, and often alone, Mihura helped condition the Spanish public so well to colloquial nonsense that by the time *The Bald Soprano* was disseminated in Spain, as one literary critic notes, Ionesco's humorous absurdities had become "a well-known thing."[20]

I   *Pre-Ionesco Absurdity*

A reading of Ionesco's highly regarded anti-play of 1950 reminds us of the tone, the spirit, and the substance of Mihura's earlier contributions to *La Codorniz*. The fourth scene of *The Bald Soprano*, for instance, offers an interesting parallel to one of Mihura's "teatrillos humorísticos" ("comic playlets") of 1942, entitled "De viaje" ("On a Journey"):

Mr. Sánchez sat in his compartment and began reading the newspaper.

Mr. Suárez, who was seated in front of Mr. Sánchez, put away his paper, which he had just finished reading, and devoted himself to admiring the landscape through the train window.

"Nice weather," said Mr. Suárez.

Mr. Sánchez answered absent-mindedly and said that indeed it was a beautiful day.

"Maybe it will also be nice in Soria," said Mr. Sánchez.

"Do you know Soria?"

"I should say so! I lived there for three years."

"Three years?" said Mr. Suárez. "Then you must know a fellow by the name of Soto."

"Amadeo Soto? Sure I know him! He runs a drugstore in the square in front of the station."

"No, no. The Soto I'm talking about is a pharmacist."

"Oh, of course! But his name isn't Amadeo! His name is Gustavo."

"That's right. You know him?"

"Very well. He was always at the get-togethers that a guy called Echave used to have."

"You know Echave?" exclaimed Mr. Suárez. "Lorenzo! Hey, he's a relative of mine!"

"Lorenzo Echave is my uncle," said Mr. Suárez.

"Your uncle?"

"Yes. He's married to Bernarda, my mother's sister."

"No kidding? Then your mother's name is Adelaida."

"You know her?"

"Of course I know her! She's my wife!"

"Your wife!" exclaimed Mr. Suárez, rocking on one foot. "Your wife? I don't believe it. Then you must be my father."

To this point Mihura's amusing dialogue resembles the classic recognition scene between Ionesco's husband-and-wife team, the Martins, in *The Bald Soprano*. They also engage in a series of interrogations and replies, of considerably greater length and with a heightened grotesquerie. Unlike Ionesco, Mihura brings complete strangers together in private conversation and consequently allows the episode an outlandish but semi-plausible base from which an absurd disclosure of blood relationship evolves. Then Mihura continues his episode beyond the humorous moment of recognition, as we perceive in the conclusion to the dialogue:

"Who would have believed it!" said Mr. Suárez, filled with emotion. "If we hadn't spoken about Soria, we would never have recognized each other."

"Soria?" asked Mr. Sánchez, stupified. "We haven't been talking about Soria. We've been speaking of Segovia."

"Segovia? You're wrong. I was talking about Soria. Evidently, there has been a misunderstanding between us. I thought you were speaking of Soria and you thought I was speaking of Segovia. Then, everything we've said has no meaning? And from the moment that it has no meaning, I am not your son?"

"Obviously! And I'm not your father. Excuse me."

"You're excused."

And Mr. Sánchez picked up his newspaper again and Mr. Suárez turned to look out the window.[21]

Mihura reverses the fortuitous discovery and returns the encounter between two strangers to the same point where it began. In contrast to the circular structure of Mihura's sketch, Ionesco's scene progresses by a growing intensification of the initial situation, ending with Mr. Martin's revelation: "Then, dear Madame, I think there's no doubt about it. We have seen one another before and you are my very wife . . . Elizabeth, I have found you!"[22]

The differences between the two renderings are minimal. Their basic features, in terms of meaning and intention, are identical. Nevertheless, despite a literary affinity, there is no concrete evidence to conclude that Ionesco engaged in a conscious appropriation of Mihura's text. Indeed, we recall that one of the charges leveled at Miguel Mihura during his directorship of *La Codorniz* was the fact that he tended to lift materials at random from Italian sources.[23]

Mihura favored the surprise recognition theme so well that he repeated it with a new focus in the April 5, 1942 issue of *La Codorniz,* reversing the former procedure of a gradual revelation leading to discovery by permitting the happy encounter of two old friends to dissolve suddenly into a realization that they had never before seen each other. Even here Mihura's intention remains the same: he parodies a common scene of reunion by the deliberate inversion of a familiar pattern. His use of commonplace utterances, juxtaposed with unusual actions, heightens the reader's apprehension of the foolishness of a universally recognized situation.

II *Original Aim of* La Codorniz

La Codorniz resisted foreclosure by never inviting the anger of Franco's regime. Its abstract formulas and absurd humor, characterized above all by a distancing from social reality, account for the magazine's uninterrupted longevity.[24] A good summation of its intended inoffensive format under Mihura's editorship is found in the following statement its founder drafted to define the purpose of the journal. This statement also provides a good insight into Mihura's philosophy of life and will be useful as we analyze his plays:

La Codorniz was born to set forth a smiling attitude to life; to divest things of their importance; to poke fun at people who take life too seriously; to get rid of irritable persons; to laugh at clichés and commonplace topics; to invent a new world, unreal and fantastic; to make people forget about the uncomfortable and disagreeable world in which they live.[25]

La Codorniz is also relevant to Mihura's later theater writings in that it contains ideas for plays he later developed for the legitimate stage. One example is the embryo for *The Case of the Gentleman Dressed in Violet* (*El caso del señor vestido de violeta*), which first appeared as a ten-minute farce in the humor magazine. Other indications of the direct influence Mihura's early writings were to have on his later creative activity for the theater are found in the bizarre skits, monologues, interviews, dialogues, and letters of *La Codorniz*. His work therein provided a valuable apprenticeship for developing comic expressions he would later employ in the avant-garde phase of his dramatic work.

CHAPTER 4

Plays of Collaboration

W HILE residing in San Sebastián during the summer of 1939,
Mihura attended literary gatherings with several aspiring
playwrights who shared his fondness for dramatic humor. Among
his fellow artists of the Café Raga's *tertulia* were Antonio de Lara,
nicknamed "Tono," and Joaquín Calvo-Sotelo. Collaborating
with each, Mihura launched his theatrical career by writing two
plays concurrently, *Long Live the Impossible* (*Viva lo imposible*)
with Calvo-Sotelo and *Neither Poor nor Rich but the Exact Reverse*
(*Ni pobre ni rico, sino todo lo contrario*) with Tono. He states that
he wrote a large portion of both plays himself as he passed from
table to table, "collaborating at one with Joaquín and at the other
with Tono."[1] Seven years later Mihura was to collaborate with
Alvaro de Laiglesia, a third member of the original café group, in
the writing of his third and final play of joint authorship, *The Case
of the Slightly Murdered Woman* (*El caso de la mujer asesinadita*).

Mihura's three plays of collaboration are revolutionary in their
scope and configuration. Each contains, with varying degrees of
effectiveness, a humor that is at once provocative, alluring, and
bizarre. On the surface, their content is not unlike the badinage
Mihura cultivated for *La Codorniz,* yet the inventive way he and
his co-authors tie the dramatic nonsense together bestows the hallmark of reliable literary value on each production. Viewed collectively, the three plays represent a new articulation of theatrical
humor in Spain. They inaugurate as well a special sense of the absurd on the Spanish stage, an absurdity of language founded on the
fusion of playful extravagance and a profound sense of humanity.

I   *A Circular Treatment of Boredom*

Long Live the Impossible, or *The Star Accountant* (*¡Viva lo imposible! o El contable de estrellas*) was first staged on the night of November 24, 1939, at Madrid's Teatro Cómico. The authors were both thirty-five years of age, though for Miguel Mihura the comedy was his first stage production, while Joaquín Calvo-Sotelo was enjoying his fifth.[2] The play was written within one month's time and lasted no longer than that in its brief opening run. A late-fall première was ill-timed. Extreme cold weather and extensive construction on Preciados Street militated against sustained commercial success. The comedy folded after only thirty performances, netting each writer fifteen hundred pesetas. Mihura decided then and there to abandon theater writing. For the next four years he busied himself with more lucrative projects. Calvo-Sotelo also turned elsewhere for remunerative employment; he did not stage another play until 1943.

Long Live the Impossible expresses the spiritual constriction of people trapped in a social milieu that disapproves of the human necessity for change, in this case an old man's spontaneous rebellion against stagnation and his difficulty in communicating to others their need to spurn the dulling effects of perpetual boredom. Don Sabino and his family, weary of conforming to rigid social norms wherein they waste away their lives in daily routine, plan to exchange the monotony of their lower middle-class existence for a life of unparalleled adventure. Their quixotic search for happiness and freedom takes them first to the sea and afterwards to an exciting circus life in the provinces. Yet the outcome we expect — life renewed and values reinstated — is totally reversed. The upshot of Don Sabino's escape from drudgery into exhilaration is to expose his family to a Romanticized form of the same kind of life they had just abandoned; their circus fling becomes as meaningless and absurd as city living. Beneath the apparent gaiety of a permissive spree they experience a bitter truth: that the assumption of a new role in life cannot change the basic configuration of a person's life. And ironically, while Don Sabino and his family try to inject uncommon excitement into their lives, the circus performers are aspiring after an ordinary, bourgeois existence. The comedy thus conveys the idea that people are thoroughly the product of the mores and the dictates of their surroundings and that the quest for change is a universal dream.

The play ends where it begins, amidst the boredom and frustration of a shabby apartment. Act One recounts Sabino's parting from ennui; Act Two depicts the family's discovery of an illusory utopian life; and Act Three returns us to their original humdrum existence. This circular construction is reinforced by other unifying devices, such as the use of parallel dialogue and music. A conversation between two unseen neighbors, chatting in an adjacent apartment in the opening scene, is repeated at the close of Act One. Likewise, a trite popular tune, whistled by another neighbor early in the play and later repeated by Sabino's son Eusebio, is reiterated with identical banality as the curtain falls. Repeated utterances and whistling lend an equilibrium of tone to the seriousness of purpose in this play, while they also bring together the opening and closing scenes in a cyclical, well-balanced pattern. Moreover, Act Three resembles Act One with its emphatic and compelling mood of sobriety, a mood which reaffirms the thoughtful spirit of the play's early action in contrast to the comparative lightness and frivolity of Act Two.

The prosaic whistled tune is more than a mere melodic appendage intended to unify action. It also provides a kind of common cosmetic base to underscore the portrayal of distressing social conditions. Penetrating through the thin walls, the whistling disturbs Eusebio, who cynically criticizes Madrid apartment living. Eusebio then whistles the same melody slightly off tune, an action which provides a thematic parallel to the sullen complaints that common household fixtures are in disrepair and the economy is unstable. Once he learns to whistle the tune correctly, Eusebio's attitude has changed; he is more cheerful, more hopeful. Indeed, this is the first hint of a wistful yearning to be free from the monotony of changelessness, a desire later symbolized by his strange fancy for an exotic gong.

Through Eusebio's actions and dialogue, we become aware that the first act of this play emphasizes with little humor the rigidity and the inanity of a particular social milieu, namely a middle-class existence in the Spanish capital. Eusebio, discontented, irritable, and indecisive, is the focal point of this treatment. Oppressed with financial and vocational concerns, he voices complaints common to his generation. He is troubled above all by the senseless requirements of his studies, requirements which cause him to be delineated as "weary," "gloomy," "melancholic," and "beleaguered," resulting ultimately in the destruction of his health and sanity.

The portrayal of Eusebio seems more indicative of Calvo-Sotelo's authorship than of Mihura's. Joaquín Calvo-Sotelo had been a state lawyer for many years. After passing the bar examinations, he pursued his profession with interest and success but gradually grew disenchanted with the career and sought novelty and excitement in the entertainment world. In Eusebio we see reflected a negative attitude toward the legal profession; he voices an indictment against the problems of entering such a career in present-day Spain: the lengthy struggle, the keen competition, burdensome lucubration, bureaucratic exigencies. His anxieties represent the common plight of all law students of his generation. The meaninglessness of his studies is made apparent as he listlessly attempts to memorize an involved municipal law dealing with state finances while the reality of acute urban taxation afflicts the household with concern and unrest. We have here an illustration of the authors' use of dramatic irony which, while it reinforces the impact of a marked social tendency in the play, also takes precedence over secondary comic meaning in dialogue or situation.

An additional example of irony in the first act is Eusebio's patching up a broken window pane with the cover of one of his law books. This action suggests a disparity between the promises of municipal law, explicitly noted in the passage Eusebio reads aloud from one of his texts; and urban fulfillment, typified by frequent allusions to material privation, indoor cold, mouse traps, and a meal consisting of beans.

Elsewhere in the comedy we encounter references to socialistic dependency upon the state and its dulling effect on personal independence. Such observations foreshadow the tone and substance of many of Calvo-Sotelo's later plays. Eusebio's impassioned exclamations, his spirit of allegation, and his sense of displeasure toward vexing situations of the present-day world are typical features of the latter playwright's productions. Nevertheless, while the content of Eusebio's discourse may adhere closely to the settled convictions and social polemics of Calvo-Sotelo's posture, it is by no means removed in spirit from the earnest but genial affirmations of Miguel Mihura's position; his own future writings will repeatedly stress the importance of securing a personal liberation from a life of habit or artificial living.

The theme of Act One is financial deprivation. Many hints of economic problems and all that they lead to, such as the necessity of carrying two jobs, the struggle for promotion, and individual desperation ending in suicide are made evident in its opening scenes. This sustained preoccupation with material gain, together with the focus on the personal despair of Eusebio, are elements which strongly suggest Calvo-Sotelo's preponderant role in the writing of Act One of *Long Live the Impossible*.

On the other hand, a winsome blend of tenderness and humor prevents the play from becoming a social documentary. Comic exaggeration is employed to point out the absurdity of conforming to the dehumanizing values of routine. An insurance agent, for example, appeals to Eusebio's desire to emulate his neighbors, who pay a higher premium each month for the privilege of having two extra horses pull the funeral wagon. Such fanciful and extravagant touches of humor, visible as well in the brief dance around Eusebio's gong, "with an air of profound pleasure," have all the earmarks of Mihurian influence.

Palmira, Eusebio's sister, represents a further clue to Mihura's role in co-authoring the work. Like the majority of Mihura's heroines. Palmira transcends a domain of subservience and restraint by dint of her personal verve and the assertion of a lively will. Though she eventually gives in to the prevailing system of values of which she is a product — through her marriage to Vicente, — she nevertheless overcomes in spirit a crass material conformity, evidenced by her consciousness of having once experienced a marvelous sense of immunity from social and moral duress.

Palmira's marital resignation conforms to the image that the Spanish woman of her day was expected to maintain. Only in a much later play of another generation does Mihura emancipate his heroine from the security and conformity of a male-dominated world, in the person of Florita of *Sublime Decision* (*Sublime decisión*; 1955). In Palmira we find Florita's spiritual forerunner — a woman unwilling to judge an individual's worth by his income. In repudiating her suitor in Act One, she rejects temporarily a society of stifling conventionality. Her escape from that monotony into the fervid activity of Act Two enlivens her sensitivity for love and deepens her compassion for human failings. Finally, her marriage to Vicente in Act Three signifies an acquiescence to the kind of world that cannot sustain her dream for adventure and freedom. And in that marriage Palmira completes her personal cycle of struggle that began as an evasion from ennui and ends with her capitulation into the same shallow existence as before. This willing compliance to the dictates of a harsh and exacting society betokens the moral import of the play. Mihura will repeat this message time and time again through the actions and reactions of his many strong female protagonists.

Vicente is the arch-villain. He is portrayed as a hateful individual, quite foreign in character to the gallery of wrongdoers in Mihura's plays who even at their worst are depicted with a modicum of human compassion and tenderness. Vicente's total absence from Act Two, that portion of the play which offers substantial evidence of Mihura's most direct and prevailing influence as co-author, suggests that this disreputable and calloused individual foretokens more closely the typical malefactor of Calvo-Sotelo's later plays, rather than the more benign perpetrators of evil in Mihura's theater. Indeed, Vicente totally lacks the capacity to dream. His values, couched in routine and regulated labor, reveal a most uninspiring example of secure mediocrity. In bearing and attitude, he resembles the kind of selfish, materialistic forces which oppose Jorge Hontanar in Calvo-Sotelo's stage masterpiece, *The Wall* (*La muralla;* 1954), or the rancor of Dalmiro Quintana in the same author's *Story of a Resentful Man* (1956).

While money and security represent the substance of Vicente's life, the antipodal position — fantasy and idealism — is maintained by Sabino, the only character capable of making a complete break from the oppressive dictates of a traditional milieu. His revolt is instantaneous and alarming, motivated by a profound hatred for the arid monotony of his existence, the common existence of the average middle-class Spaniard:

Let's break with it all. Let's abandon our posts. And let's take flight! Down with the norm, the rule, and the anticipated! ... Long live the impossible! ...

Don Sabino's new creed. is a declaration of emancipation from drudgery. It is sufficiently insurgent in spirit to have caused the entire play to be deleted from Mihura's first volume of complete plays.[3]

The presentation of Don Sabino is characteristic of Mihura's ingratiating characters. Moreover, Sabino's first appearance on stage corresponds to a dramatic manner that is undeniably Mihurian.

When he enters the apartment in Act One, his mien and language are the complete opposite of what the audience and the other characters anticipate. This device of startling the spectator momentarily through surprise is frequently employed by Mihura in most of his plays. It contributes to the complex of ironic contrasts underlying the dramatic action. Surprise happenings constitute a fundamental aspect of the plot development in his theater.[4] An interesting thematic parallel in Mihura's writings is the circus atmosphere in the second act of *Long Live the Impossible* and the appearance of unusual circus performers in Act Two of *Three Top Hats* (*Tres sombreros de copa*). Like Benavente before him, Mihura also discovered the dramatic possibilities inherent in the spectacle of the circus or the music hall. The choice was most appropriate, for Spain was reputedly the circus capital of Europe from 1920 to 1956.[5]

Another parallel is the unrealized love affair between Palmira and Fede and the comparable involvement between Paula and Dionisio. Fede's preoccupation with financial security, while serving as a thematic parallel to Vicente's own concern for material comfort in the same play, also tokens the kind of life and attitudes Don Sacramento and his family represent in *Three Top Hats*. Eusebio's weak and contradictory nature, which surprisingly assumes in Act Two the appearance of solid resolution, only to degenerate in Act Three to a regrettable state of renunciation and defeat, resembles that of the vacillating, weak-willed Dionisio, who voluntarily submits to a life of inevitable vulgarity in leaving Paula to marry Margarita. The focal point of the two plays is identical at this juncture; a confrontation between two contrasting milieux dominates both plots and constitutes the basic idea behind each comedy. On the one side we have a narrow-minded, habituary existence (Vicente = Don Sacramento); on the other, a free, artistic way of life (Sabino = Paula).

Just as Palmira and Fede represent two entirely different worlds in *Long Live the Impossible,* so Paula and Dionisio are contrasted by their respective backgrounds. Virtually all the characters in *Long Live the Impossible* are trying to flee from an enfeebling ennui; they enter a brief but falsified replica of their dreams, analogous to Dionisio's attempt to gain freedom from a life without color or promise. Palmira is torn between two men, Dionisio between two women. Vicente accuses Don Sabino of being a bohemian, as does Don Sacramento accuse Dionisio.

Perhaps the most impressive similarity is found in Palmira's symbolic releasing of the dove at the close of Act Two in *Long Live the Impossible,* a gesture which signifies her personal resolve to forsake the quest, abandon the circus, and return to a life of domestic monotony. This action can be compared to the dramatic toss of the three top hats, a symbol of Paula's resistance to self-pity and her resolve to return to her former way of life, unfettered by sentimental, emotional ties.

The fact that multiple similarities between the two plays can be cited lends credence to two suppositions. First, Mihura's collaboration with Calvo-Sotelo was more than incidental. His influence — through style, subject matter, treatment, and humor — predominates in virtually all of Act Two. Second, the fact that Mihura had written but had not been able to produce *Three Top Hats* may have tempted him to incorporate parallel elements from the manuscript of his 1932 composition into the later production, assured a professional staging owing to Calvo-Sotelo's established reputation in playwriting. Mihura was in fact sorely disenchanted by the extreme wariness shown *Three Top Hats* by various promoters; his personal writings convey a sense of apprehension over the ultimate destiny of his silenced work.[6] Perhaps he took advantage in collaborating with Calvo-Sotelo to salvage some of the outstanding features of his manuscript play, allowing the circus episode of Act Two of *Long Live the Impossible* to become a literary counterpart to the music hall proceedings of *Three Top Hats.*

Above all, the underlying message of the play, echoed and re-echoed in each of the three acts, but dramatized most poignantly by the elements of contrast, humor, and surprise in Act Two, is typically Mihurian; it inaugurates the kind of philosophical posture he will assume in his subsequent productions, namely, that life is incomplete without a capacity for adventure and an individual exertion to realize one's dreams. This thought is expressly developed through the discourse and actions of Sabino, who states on two occasions the unmistakable moral lesson of *Long Live the Impossible:* "Failing to arrive is not a sin. Failing to depart is.... Happiness lies only in being what one has wanted to be."[7]

Our brief analysis of *Long Live the Impossible* demonstrates that Mihura's first published play was intellectual and literary in scope and spirit. The gaiety of tone and the winsome humor of Act

Two are particularly ascribable to him, while the more somber social undertones of Acts One and Three resemble the moral pronouncements of Calvo-Sotelo's theater. By returning the spectator in Act Three to the same inanity portrayed ten years earlier in Act One, the playwrights make manifest the sad results of blind conformity to the tedium of everyday activities. Void of the sustaining force of imagination and decisive action, this conformity produces unremitting frustration and triteness in the lives of many human beings.[8] Sabino alone transcends the debilitating forces of habit; significantly he does so on a New Year's Eve, taking his grandson with him, thus signifying that the individual struggle of a former generation bestows hope and promise of emancipation upon a future age. The problem is treated seriously. The dialogue is consistent with characterization. The plot line is clear and logical. And the play conveys a pertinent message which, while applying no doubt to post-war Spain, is nonetheless free from topical or regionalistic expressions; it has a vitality and universality typically Mihurian. *Long Live the Impossible* warrants serious respect as the first play of a young, promising dramatist.

II   *A Venture into the Absurd*

Mihura was keenly sensitive to the commercial failure of his first stage production. When *Long Live the Impossible* closed in mid-December of 1939, he turned to writing short stories and humorous articles and drew sketches for Spanish periodicals. He also earned a good income as a script writer for Spanish films. Meanwhile, he reluctantly completed writing the third act to a play which he and Tono had begun in the summer of 1939. Upon the play's completion, the authors decided to sell it to an international movie producer named Benito Perojo, who intended to film *Neither Poor nor Rich but the Exact Reverse* (*Ni pobre ni rico, sino todo lo contrario*) in Argentina. When, after a four-year delay, the movie had not yet appeared, Tono insisted that the new play be recalled inasmuch as its humor seemed all the more current and promised an enormous commercial triumph. The popular magazine, *La Codorniz,* had appeared in 1941, creating a propitious climate for the incongruous humor of the unproduced play.

Mihura cared nothing for the work. He feared that its revival might damage his and Tono's reputation in their journalistic careers. To some extent he was right. While the repurchasing of the play ultimately brought fame to both playwrights, the immediate consequences of this action were most unpleasant. In the first place, Mihura's reluctance to stage the play engendered a breach with Tono. Their subsequent mutual enmity, exploited and exaggerated by the press, lasted throughout the play's rehearsals, performances, and for several ensuing years.[9] Secondly, the play itself fomented a controversy of unusual magnitude. On the one hand, spectators either stamped their feet indignantly or gave the disquieting comedy a standing ovation. On the other hand, critical acclaim was either laudatory to the extreme or of damning rejection. One critic, for example, extolled the production in these beatific words: "It taught me how beauty can rise from the strings of a harp high into the heavens."[10] In contrast, Emilio Morales de Acevedo was quoted as having disdained the work with a shrug and the comment: "I've not lived long enough to understand this."[11]

Mihura explains in his lengthy Introduction to *Three Top Hats* that the polemics became distressingly vehement and divided public sentiment into two camps: those who favored the humorous absurdities of *La Codorniz,* of which Mihura was then editor, and those who repudiated the magazine as the project of a madman.[12] Both schools of thought troubled Mihura, who disliked seeing the play linked to the familiar *humor codornicesco* (*Codorniz*-style humor), when the magazine had first appeared two full years after the writing of his and Tono's comedy.

The notoriety which the play received did not prevent its being a tremendous box-office failure. It failed both in Madrid and in Barcelona. The drama critic Torrente Ballester points out that during the time in which *Neither Poor nor Rich* and *The Case of the Slightly Murdered Woman* were premiered, the Teatro María Guerrero, where the two plays were first staged, was a theater catering to authors whose plays had been rejected by promoters, and therefore paid admission was only infrequently exacted from the public. Torrente states: "Those exceptional plays were not fully understood. People paid attention only to the strange humor with which they were written, and the same things which annoyed them about *La Codorniz* also annoyed them about the dialogue ... of those two plays."[12] Evaristo Acevedo adds that the abstract humor of Mihura and Tono's writings did not penetrate the psychology of their spectators, "who preferred the concrete and critical humor that other playwrights cultivated."[13]

Mihura, chagrined by the publicity given to his quarrel with Tono, distressed over the hapless commercial fiasco of their play, and perturbed at the apparent lack of objectivity and understanding accorded his novel and revolutionary brand of humor, abandoned the theater for a second time. In Barcelona, where *Neither Poor nor Rich* was poorly received, Mihura was asked the following questions in a newspaper interview. The playwright's replies are most significant, for they represent his first declaration of divorce from an avant-garde posture in the theater:

"Are you satisfied with *Neither Poor nor Rich?*"

"No. I consider this work to be only an experiment. This type of theater has ended with this effort. For my part, I don't intend to write another work of this type."

"But you will continue to write plays?"

"For the moment, no. I'll wait until the popularity and the mode of this humor, and the controversy created by *Neither Poor nor Rich* have died away, so that people can go to see my other play without any emotion and without prejudices of any kind. Moreover, both those who criticize as well as those who defend *La Codorniz* would expect from me another work of this style, and I intend to write something entirely different...."[14]

Mihura's disappointment was due largely to the financial setback resulting from the rejection of his first two plays. A mild note of cynicism, coupled with an apparent sense of insecurity and defensiveness, attends other comments he made in interviews recorded prior to the première of his first successful play, *Three Top Hats*. His prose writings of this early period, particularly the Introduction to *Three Top Hats* (1943) and *My Memoirs* (1943–44), are also flavored with a cynical wit that does not conceal a defensive attitude toward unfavorable evaluations from critics, promoters, and the general public. The underlying source for Mihura's tempered pessimism may likely be the small returns for his efforts. He frankly admits that the greater financial remuneration he obtained following the extraordinary success of *Three Top Hats* prompted his decision to remain in dramaturgy.

Mihura came to realize that his financial security as a professional playwright would be tenuous unless he made concessions to the tastes and demands of his promoters and public. In the opinion of many reputable drama critics who have declared Mihura's avant-garde period to be his best theater, this was an unfortunate decision, for it compromised a unique form of dramatic art in favor of the opportunistic attainment of commercial profit.

The farcical humor of *Neither Poor nor Rich* resides in its use of verbal nonsense to satirize the fact that communication between human beings is in a process of gradual deterioration and that the senseless conventions of inconsequential speech are producing a yawning gulf between language and reality. Abelardo, a wealthy but insecure young man, has been rejected by Margarita, whose pride outweighs her poverty to such an extent that she spurns her rich suitor out of fear that people will think she has married him for his money. He therefore decides to forsake all his wealth in order to win her affection. He purchases useless inventions, engages thieves to burglarize his home, and gambles away his money. At last he is ruined, but Margarita now rejects him because he is penniless. Through the aid of his friend, the Baroness, Abelardo regains most of his wealth. His earlier sympathetic acquaintance with the world of penury prompts him to found a union of beggars, known as The Poor Trust Company. This action further increases his personal yearning for the freedom that a life of vagrancy offers. Believing in the end that a voluntary repudiation of all his material possessions, social commitments, habits, hobbies, and prejudices will assure him that degree of happiness he is seeking, Abelardo goes off to live like a vagabond on the river bank, catching fish and enjoying the sun in a life of jovial abandon.

The play's uniqueness inheres in its extravagant, absurd, and startling humor, a humor that bears no small resemblance to the unconventional lines of comic farce found in such playwrights as Enrique García Álvarez, Pedro Muñoz Seca, and Enrique Jardiel Poncela. The total inverisimilitude of this work, with its lacerating satire against timeworn situations and tired clichés, has endeared it to such critics as Alfredo Marqueríe, Domingo Pérez Minik, and Emilio Clocchiatti.[15] The play bears a remarkable resemblance to certain characteristics which have in more recent years been ascribed to the theater of Eugène Ionesco. Like the French-Romanian playwright, Mihura and Tono also deal with "the tragic spectacle of human life reduced to passionless automatism through bourgeois convention and the fossilization of language."[16] *Neither Poor nor Rich* is an overt satire on the use of clichés; in attacking the absurdity and falseness of the commonplace in language, it makes use of the same resources which Esslin attributes to Ionesco's *The Bald Soprano, The Lesson,* and *The Chairs,* namely, the abandonment of discursive logic and the reduction of verbal communication to meaningless patter.[17]

But while the admixture of triviality, platitudes, and dislocated dialogue in Mihura and Tono's work approximates Ionesco's exploitation of the syllogistic structure of language, any other similarities to subsequent productions within the absurdist tradition can only be considered coincidental. Mihura and Tono are not absurdists but precursors; their play might well be considered a prelude to certain elements of the absurd in Western dramatic literature.

Unlike many works of Ionesco and Beckett, where identities are often confused, distorted, or lost, Mihura's characters are "endowed with a cohesion and an interdependence"[18] that make them singular creatures of a unique, esoteric world. They do suffer a process of dehumanization, but only to the degree whereby they allow the rhetorical nature of dead language to render them incapable of intelligent action. For instance, the personalities of Abelardo, Margarita, the Baroness, and Abelardo's servant Julio are neither destroyed nor sacrificed before a surprising concatenation of absurd utterances, yet their authenticity as human beings is devalued as a consequence of their having adopted a fossilized debris of clichés. That their basic unity and consistency as characters remain intact is a credit to Mihura and Tono's craftsmanship.

The collaborators have deliberately applied the mechanics of language to nullify full credibility of character. The ready-made expressions which the main characters use are intended not merely to typify by means of dialogue, but to convey the essential disintegration of human communication into the empty platitudes of everyday discourse: "One must free himself from words," affirms José Monleón commenting on the significance of *Neither Poor nor Rich.* "The spoken word is, from this perspective, an expression of automatism, of irrationality, of slavery," all arising from an excess of impoverished language.[19] In Mihura's later play, *Carlota,* this same idea is suggested. One of the characters defines the attitude by the remark: "it seemed as though we spoke using a conversation manual,"[20] a statement that also calls to mind the intended parody of Ionesco's first play.

Margarita's incurable stupidity illustrates the result of allowing senseless words to dull the spirit. She represents a stubborn middle-class resistance to original thought. Through Abelardo's romantic tributes paid to her early in Act One, we anticipate meeting a woman of principle, but in a manner typical of Mihurian plays, her appearance and behavior invalidate our former expectations. She is prejudiced, fickle, infantile, and basically materialistic. Her principles are merely phrases that she once learned by heart. She is illogical, unpredictable, and contradictory, a product of a world of shallow thinking and self-interest.

Abelardo is not without his own repertory of absurdities. Before his liberation he is somewhat like the weak-willed Dionisio of *Three Top Hats,* all too prone to adopt the contagious conventions and ideas of his surroundings. With every vacillating word and action, he reveals the frustration of one who struggles to overcome contradiction and paradox. As the pivotal character of the play, Abelardo is affected by the absurd behavior of everyone else. The other characters contribute "nonsense, uselessness, arbitrary acts, and all that serves no purpose,"[21] a credo he eventually accepts as the one true reality of life.

The equally dreamy and distracted Baroness is one of the characters who disarms Abelardo the most. She does so by her contrary logic, her criticism of Abelardo's own use of cliché, and her personal use of common expressions in an absurd context. Julio, Abelardo's stuffy, conventional servant, whose propriety renders him void of human sympathy, serves a comic function as a contrast to the madness of his master. Although Abelardo tries to persuade Julio to smell a bouquet of flowers, hoping the experience will enervate his priggish attitude and make him more humane, the servant is unwilling: "I won't smell them. I'm an honorable man."[22] He is very much like the conformist Vicente in *Long Live the Impossible* and the orthodox Don Sacramento in *Three Top Hats.* In the end, however, Julio transfers his own identity to Abelardo's; he too adopts eccentricity in an effort to be rid of ritualistic conformity. The final scene finds him walking across the stage, dressed as a beggar, carrying bread crumbs in a cone.

This conversion of the former snob into a vagabond unveils the basic meaning behind Mihura and Tono's play. By upholding and favoring a bohemian posture, supported by the arbitrary and the absurd in human action, the playwrights imply the meaninglessness of that reality we accept as a reasonable and organized pattern of human existence, and thus they subscribe to a liberating departure into the gratuitous realm of inconsistency, nonconformity, and utter nonsense in order to enhance the joy of living. Consequently, *Neither Poor nor Rich* enjoys a close affinity with the purport and spirit of *Long Live the Impossible* and *Three Top Hats*. The three comedies may be said to form a trilogy in which the stylized and stereotyped comportment of the upper and middle classes in society are placed in confrontation with the free-thinking and unconventional world, resulting in a satire on the former way of life and an endorsement for the latter.

The play also employs other elements of the absurd besides language distortions. Among these is an outpouring of unusual objects on stage. In *Long Live the Impossible* the exhibition of curious articles includes an oriental gong, a clown playing a violin, and numerous trappings connected with the circus environment. Though striking for their novelty and exciting as unique stage props, none of the uncommon objects in the Calvo-Sotelo and Mihura production appear without logical, verbal, or thematic preparation. In contrast, the strange things which spring forth in both *Neither Poor nor Rich* and *Three Top Hats* are entirely unexpected and bear little or no relationship to stage action or dialogue. Such items appear with a regularity just short of the kind of proliferation usually associated with Ionesco's theater.

In Act One, for instance, three inventors are engaged with Abelardo in the longest sustained dialogue of the absurd to be found in Mihura's theater. The scene is reminiscent of Jardiel, whose plays often abound in outlandish accessories. One inventor carries a harp and a large automobile klaxon, but neither instrument is capable of making any noise. The second has a saw that sounds a bell when its work is finished; he tests his invention by sawing the legs off a table in the room, but the bell fails to work. The third reveals an electric apparatus for peeling potatoes, though it can peel but one solitary potato before breaking down, never to work again. Later, in another scene, the Baroness enters, carrying a portable gramophone and records that never leave her side. On one occasion she pulls a loaf of bread out of her pocket, an act similar to the sudden and surprising appearance of foreign objects in Act Two of *Three Top Hats*. Other examples in this category include the flowers that Abelardo frequently carries in either or both hands; the arrival of three thieves in a car with a mule; the appearance of trumpets, hatchets, ladders, and hoses with four firemen; the emergence of the Baroness' chauffeur displaying a flag; and the silent stroll across the stage by Julio, wearing a derby and carrying a paper cornucopia teeming with bread crumbs.

Even normal objects are misidentified, misused, or accorded an absurd dimension. Abelardo moves time ahead by turning forward the hands on his clock; the Baroness starts to exit by the window; Margarita attempts to relocate the natural setting of a city park as though she were rearranging house furniture; her stupid aunt mistakes a typewriter for a piano, then remarks upon typing how woefully out of tune it is. These and other instances of the humor of incongruity suggest connections with vaudeville and the slapstick farces of the Marx Brothers. Indeed, one of the chief characteristics of the absurd theater of the post-war period is that it borrows objects for scenic and comic effects from the circus, from the *commedia dell'arte* and from the comedy of the music hall.

Mihura obviously has a penchant for this tradition, for we encounter the appearance of unfamiliar phenomena in many of his plays. It is most common in *Three Top Hats*. The tendency is likewise noted in *Carlota,* where the detective Harris pulls out a steaming cup of tea from his coat pocket. The final act of *Miracle at the López House* (*Milagro en casa de los López*) includes the unwarranted and somewhat preposterous appearance of a girl in a bikini followed by the materialization of a transparent angel, both emerging from behind the living room draperies.

The linguistic absurdities in *Neither Poor nor Rich* are likely forerunners of similar language in the absurdist writings of the early 1950's. Among these elements in Mihura and Tono's work we find a breakdown of plausible associations and a loss of precise terms and attributes. Ruptures in phraseology, for example, invite incongruency and elicit laughter.[22] Properties which normally correspond to one thing or can only apply to a particular linguistic mold are transferred to a totally unlike object or are improperly rendered, so that natural understanding is hampered and the playful banter of the comedy is furthered. Francisco de Cossio observed on the night of its première that this play heralded the surrealism of humor on the Spanish stage.[23]

With regard to absurd reversals of anticipated behavior, the following summarized situations will suffice to delineate further the absurdist spirit of *Neither Poor nor Rich*: Abelardo schedules

three thieves to rob his home. He insists they do so rapidly or he
will phone the police. He asks them not to make any noise and to
leave carefully so they will not be apprehended. Later a group of
firemen appear for another of Abelardo's appointments. They
casually sit down, take a drink, and ask ridiculous questions while
the house is blazing. They aid the progress of the fire by throwing
match books and furniture into the flames. Their domestic nonchalance foreshadows — if only by coincidence — the unusual
appearance of the firemen in Ionesco's *The Bald Soprano.*

Reversals in physical attire are also common. Characters first
dressed as aristocrats appear later as vagabonds. Incongruous behavior accompanies their change. Abelardo, a beggar in Act Two,
gives five centavos to the wealthy Don Cristino. An authentic
pauper whistles a difficult operatic air. Three noble ladies have a
picnic on the park lawn with Abelardo and his beggar friends.
Finally, the vagabonds themselves organize a syndicate and undertake to draft the city's vagrants into a prosperous union.[24]

Like other successful satires that depend upon deviation, inco-
herence, and incongruity to elucidate the human condition, Mihura
and Tono's work offers insights analogous to life. By following its
own laws of logic, the play demonstrates a coherent purpose. It is
understandable, though, why *Neither Poor nor Rich* and *La
Codorniz* ignited public furor. Both enterprises — the one dramatic, the other journalistic — anticipated by some ten years the
spirit of the absurd in contemporary literature. Their impact has
added a new direction to Spanish humoristic literature. However,
to designate this play as a legitimate part of the absurdist repertory
requires one basic qualification. *Neither Poor nor Rich* is not a
philosophic reflection on the absurdity of human existence. It is not
a play of ideas whose subject matter is somber, violent, or bitter. Its
dialogue discloses no evidence of an all-prevailing sense of anguish
at the disintegration of individuals in a world in decomposition.
Man's isolation and spiritual dereliction, so frequently encountered
in the French absurdist writers of the 1950's, is nowhere suggested
in Mihura and Tono's play. Nihilism, existential despair, and the
psychic annihilation of the individual are totally absent. Consequently, inasmuch as the Spanish playwrights are not concerned
with the enigmatic aspects of being, their work cannot be weighed
in the same balance with such plays as *The Bald Soprano, The
Chairs,* and *Endgame,* where man is depicted as truly divorced

from his transcendental roots.

One must admit a diversity of method and form within the tradition of the absurd, for the theater of the absurd itself is, after all, merely a term applied by critics, editors, and historians of literature, in labeling a group of authors who rarely, if ever, apply the term "absurdist" to themselves.[25] "What is sometimes labeled the absurd," writes Eugène Ionesco, "is only the denunciation of the ridiculous nature of a language which is empty of substance, sterile, made up of clichés and slogans."[26] In this respect, Mihura and Tono play a significant role in the tradition of the absurd. By virtue of their avant-garde venture of 1939 into this domain, they stand among the precursors of a rich and variegated trend in twentieth-century literature, and they can claim the undisputed honor of having inaugurated a special sense of the absurd on the Spanish stage.

III   *Toward a Conservative Posture*

Two years after the staging of *Neither Poor nor Rich,* Mihura was obliged by financial necessity to write a new play. The basic idea for its plot was already clear in his mind when, one morning in the fall of 1945, he encountered his young friend Álvaro de Laiglesia in the Madrid tavern, Cervecería de Correos. Laiglesia, now twenty-three years of age, had assumed managership of *La Codorniz* only one year before. He was so enthusiastic over Mihura's idea that he immediately accepted a casual invitation to collaborate with Don Miguel in writing the play.[27]

Upon its completion, the play, entitled *The Case of the Slightly Murdered Woman* (*El caso de la mujer asesinadita*), was read to several friends in Barcelona — actors, directors, and other playwrights, — all of whom advised the authors to reduce the jokes and to eliminate clever word play.[28] Mihura was appalled. He had deliberately set out to divert, to amuse, to fill the strange and puzzling action of his comedy with "pleasing lines" that would satisfy the public's taste for an entertainment supercharged with humor. Nevertheless, he and Laiglesia complied. They purged the play of its surface pleasantries, preparing it for a February première in Madrid's María Guerrero Theater.

The public's reaction and the critical response to this new production disconcerted Mihura because the work, like his former plays, was labeled "strange and imposing," "*codornicesca,*" and "avant-garde" by those who celebrated its artistic merits. And this response ignored the authors' efforts to alert their audience that the play had nothing whatever to do with *La Codorniz.*[29] The public was apparently conditioned to anticipate a style of humor known by the absurd nature of its language. The mere fact that the first editor of *La Codorniz* and his successor had collaborated on the same play was sufficient evidence to persuade the vast majority of playgoers that the work was intimately and irrevocably linked with the popular humor magazine. Many thus entered the theater with a preconceived notion and interpreted everything they saw as the obvious confirmation of their expectations.

Mihura recorded his dismay as follows: "What I thought to be a work for general consumption almost resulted in an avant-garde writing. . . . I was tremendously upset and ceased thinking about theater writing."[30] His disillusionment concerning what he considered an unwarranted classification of the play as a staged extension of *La Codorniz* was further aggravated when the entire production brought him the trifling sum of 12,000 pesetas.[31] Mihura therefore forsook the theater for six years. In the interim, he earned a small fortune in the film industry. Upon his return to playwriting with the success of *Three Top Hats,* he firmly repudiated the *codornicesco* tradition of his avant-garde humor; thereafter he would affirm over and again the formula that since 1952 has characterized his commercial triumphs and personal prosperity: "There is only one way to proceed in the theater: staging plays that please, performed by actors who command interest."[32]

The comedy concerns, quite simply, the calculated double murder of Mercedes and Norton, a wife and her lover, at the hands of the husband Lorenzo and his secretary Raquel. A complicated web of suspense, with scenes shifting in and out of reality, attends the dramatic game. A full résumé of the plot is unnecessary; although the play consists of a single action, its intricate pattern of flashbacks governed by a complex dream sequence and the constant interchange of the unreal with the real, the realm of fantasy fused with the normal world of casual events, obfuscate any reasonable attempt to isolate details for a full understanding of the developing mystery. Suffice it to say that the play's comic elements lie precisely in these multiple contrasts between the theme of suspense and the light, sometimes frivolous, tone of the authors' treatment. In the end the murderers, who killed in order to remarry, are themselves victims of a boring, insipid union. Once again Mihura parades a favorite message of his, written with a dash of bitterness and pungent sarcasm, that marital bliss is a myth.

The Slightly Murdered Woman is a work of transition in the evolution of Mihura's theater. It represents a mid-way point in the author's voluntary effort to shift his stage aesthetics from an appeal to the cultured, sophisticated minority, to a theater designed for a sizeable middle-class audience. Among all his early writings, this play best betokens his conversion from unfettered spontaneity to the adoption of a conventional and compromising attitude. The play differs from Mihura's former productions by virtue of its technical superiority and its perfectly structured intrigue. Despite its having been written in only twenty days, the play reveals an extraordinary ingenuity of construction. The frequent turns of its action from fantasy to reality and back again to the world of hallucinations are managed with the ease of sound intelligence and with an air of polished sophistication.

José Monleón designates the work "a pirouette of great formal preciosity," observing that in his opinion "there are very few works in the Spanish theater that are constructed with so much dexterity."[33] Torrente Ballester likewise extols the play for its "perfect construction."[34] Its highly structured intrigue has earned the comedy considerable recognition internationally. It broke a record in Mexico City, for example, when it reached its 415th performance in 1964.[35]

The Slightly Murdered Woman contains none of the strange verbal dislocations or distortions common to Mihura's other plays of collaboration. Its language is simple, sober, and natural, though repeatedly irrelevant. Some episodes are clearly shorn of humor; their inconsequential dialogue, while elegant and credible, evinces Mihura and Laiglesia's endeavor to divest the work of excessive humor.

This is one of the few plays in Mihura's repertory to achieve its effectiveness through means other than dialogue. A predominance of spiritualistic elements comprises its most cogent appeal. In an atmosphere already rarefied with puzzling and mysterious tones, owing to constant reminders about a murder and the intricate fusion of dreams with reality, the focus is wrested from the cleverness and fluidity of the characters' speech toward the surface action.

Alfredo Marquerie lists the various themes concerning occultism in this unique work as follows: "... themes of terror and metaphysics, telepathy, premonition, divinations of the inner world of dreams, spiritualism, phantom appearances, and chiromancy."[36] Add to this list the attendant theme of adultery, incorporated within the context of the murder episode, and one can readily understand why in 1946 the play was labeled by one reactionary Italian reporter as "a work whose moral aspect is most unfortunate, ... dangerous for all spectators."[37] This same critic, however, concurred with the majority of noted Spanish reviewers in admitting that these distrusted recondite elements exemplify in a literary sense "a notable effort to carry the theater through the difficult course of art and novelty."[38]

The novelty spoken of here is the very attribute that motivated one writer to declare that the play contains a definite avant-garde feature, being "free of conventional fetters and the mediocre prevailing customs that almost smother our theater." [39] This uniqueness is evident in the recurring parallelism which the authors sustain in all three acts of the play. They juxtapose a serious and precise reality with a whimsical taste of the supernatural. The real world of romance and intrigue blends indistinguishably into an unreal world characterized by seances, ghosts, and divination.

Most of Act One, for example, is pervaded by the enigmatic incidents of a single dream superimposing its own reality upon the reality of life. This dream sequence is reiterated in Act Two and the gradual realization of its fatalistic tidings made more and more apparent. A second dream confirms the first, and reality consists once again of the concurrence of normal fact and supernatural events. Realistic action is further complicated by the appearance of two old people dressed in mourning who have been dead for five years. In Act Three the previous dreams merge into a meaningful context of factual existence. Prophecy is fulfilled with the deaths of Mercedes and Norton, and their spiritual union restores the supernatural theme. Just as fantasy appears to replace reality in the terminal scene, the action shifts again to disclose the real-life boredom of Raquel and Lorenzo, whose roles are exempt from the excitement and exhilaration of transcendental occurrences.

The play clearly partakes of the same atmosphere that characterizes Noel Coward's *Blithe Spirit* (1941), a play that was breaking all records in London at the same time *The Slightly Murdered Woman* was performed in Madrid. Coward's work, as Fernández de Asís points out, differs considerably in terms of the plot line; the correspondence is merely one of "an identical spirit ... of the times."[40] It is interesting to note that Jorge de la Cueva finds a resemblance in the appearance of the old deceased couple in Act Two to the entrance of the Heavenly Policemen in Ferenc Molnar's *Liliom* (1909).[41] Yet another critic observes a likeness between the carefree chatter in Joseph Kesselring's *Arsenic and Old Lace* (1941) in the scene concerning the preparation of the deadly poison, and the corresponding incident in Act Two of Mihura and Laiglesia's play.[42] Díez Crespo finds an echo of Cocteau in the soft accent of mystery lying beneath a clear plot.[43] These are all peripheral resemblances, of course, and in no way suggest direct literary influence. Marqueríe is quick to point out that while Mihura responds to a theme in vogue in Western films and literature, *The Case of the Slightly Murdered Woman* "is of a total and absolute originality ... that seeks its inspiration in the zone of the unusual and the disquieting."[44]

The first act also contains elements reminiscent of the kind of absurdity associated with Mihura's earlier writings. The appearance of Norton as an American Indian, for instance, has been interpreted as a sign of surface nonsense. Professor Theodore S. Beardsley objects to Mihura's Indian as "a loose, disturbing, untied thread" in a play that is "otherwise too tidy to allow us to assume that this is not a calculated technique."[45] The Indian, however, is simply an expressionistic element existing in the dream world of Mercedes, who conjures up many unusual details to accompany the true omen of her impending murder. The Indian functions to reduce the lucidity of her dream and to graft a fabricated element of illogical distortion upon an otherwise normal action. This is a procedure typical of Mihura in his early theater and contributes to the linking of this play with earlier comedies. Another unusual figment of Mercedes' imagination, reproduced as though it were a realistic happening, is the maid's first-scene exit carrying a bird cage with a canary in it, followed by her immediate re-entrance carrying the same cage that now contains a cat. Mercedes also dreams that her servants are haughty and insubordinate to her, a notion which provides an amusing contrast after the dream when we note how obsequious and gentle is their manner in real life.

The title of the play suggests one additional reason to justify the tendency of critics to include *The Slightly Murdered Woman* in Mihura's avant-garde period. The diminutive appended to *asesinada* catches us off guard; we are amused at the thought of a woman being "a little bit murdered."[46] By entitling their play in this manner, Mihura and Laiglesia are merely responding to a popular trend of their day. A surprisingly large number of plays of the post-Civil War era are distinguished by a humor of incongruity in their titles. Jardiel Poncela engages in this practice often, as illustrated by the comedies *Blondes Go Better with Potatoes* and *Four Hearts in Check and Backward March*. After writing *Neither Poor nor Rich but the Exact Reverse* with Mihura, Tono continued to employ incongruous titles, as in *William Hotel* and *Pluperfect Crime*. Laiglesia playfully produced such titles as *There Are No Clams in Heaven* and *You Too Were Born Quite Naked*.

Another popular trend that gained impetus during the 1940's and blossomed enormously during the next decade was the writing of mystery plays, or dramatized detective novels. Mihura's several "case" plays are not all comedies of intrigue, as their titles might suggest, but they do exemplify the author's propensity to cultivate plays of this familiar genre. *Carlota, A No-Account Woman* (*Una mujer cualquiera*), *Peaches and Syrup* (*Melocotón en almíbar*) and *The Decent Woman* (*La decente*) are his best-known contributions to that provocative class of theater known in Spain as *el género policíaco* ("the detective genre").

The Slightly Murdered Woman partakes of this climate. Throughout the play new notes of mystery and suspense are constantly interjected. Because a criminal act is imminent from the beginning, the element of time becomes important to the action; the position or location of physical objects takes on an added significance; the entrances and exits of all major characters become essential to our interest in the plot's development. Overall, there is a paradoxically light-hearted feeling of impending doom. Instead of pity and fear, we experience a sense of amusement at the action and astonishment before the many supernatural resources Mihura and Laiglesia evoke to flavor their satire.

Through the magic of humor, upheld in this work in the roles of Mercedes and Norton, the authors control the intrigue within an atmosphere of subdued jocularity. Thus it is that the play can make a valid spoof on the tediousness of a dull marriage and can lampoon occult practices within the framework of a clever and stirring mystery drama that introduces the serious themes of infidelity and homicide.

Finally, the play offers a thematic parallel to both previous and forthcoming Mihurian productions. As in many of his other plays, nearly everyone in this comedy is bored to death. All major resolves in the action are made out of tedium. Mercedes, the protagonist, is presented to us with the "absent and romantic air" of one who, "to avoid excessive boredom in her marriage, amuses herself by reading adventure novels and by giving the maids a bad time."[47] Her indifferent relationship with her husband Lorenzo grows increasingly colorless until, albeit a victim of his scheming, she finds in death a welcome relief from boredom. Rosaura, the fat cook, also gives utterance to her boredom. She prefers to live in a world of make-believe, fearing the dullness of her life will drive her insane. Renato, the gardener, expresses the boredom he also feels: "I'm fed up with pruning the trees, watering the garden, and looking at the sky without knowing why ...."[48] Lorenzo, too, is bored, particularly with his listless wife. He is characterized as unimaginative, dull, and stupid. Though he murders Mercedes to find freedom and felicity with Raquel, he discovers nothing but absolute boredom in Raquel's presence. For now that the adventure of a secret liaison has ended, his life is again dreary and dull. The final stage directions bring the action to a fitting close with two lazy yawns:

> In an armchair, doing needlework, sits Raquel. She is wearing Mercedes' evening gown. In another armchair, reading a newspaper, sits Lorenzo.... Both have the appearance of total boredom. Raquel yawns. Lorenzo yawns. The curtain falls.[49]

We have seen how *The Case of the Slightly Murdered Woman* represents a partial departure from Mihura's revolutionary theater of humor. Consciously aware of their craft, Mihura and Laiglesia endeavor to weave a humor of situation within the framework of a serious theme. That spontaneity of dialogue, so characteristic of Mihura's former writings, is not apparent in the thoughtful, though playful, technical achievement of *The Slightly Murdered Woman*. This comedy contains echoes of the sincerity and boldness of Mihura's former plays but reveals as well a willful gravitation toward the formulation of a conservative posture. Quite simply, Mihura desires, now and henceforth, to please his public.

CHAPTER 5

Two Worlds in Vital Confrontation

*T*hree Top Hats (*Tres sombreros de copa*) is the play that has earned Miguel Mihura his greatest distinction in the contemporary European theater. Its staging in 1952 created a sensation in the Spanish theater world, and, as one translation followed upon another, Mihura was swiftly catapulted into international renown as one of Spain's outstanding humorists.

This play alone, according to José Monleón, would have sufficed to establish Mihura as an important author of contemporary drama.[1] Ricardo Domenech values the comedy on a plane equal in importance to the *esperpentos* (grotesque farces) of Valle-Inclán, the *greguerías* (humorous metaphors) of Ramón Gómez de la Serna, and the entire theater of Enrique Jardiel Poncela, as representing "the Spanish contribution to the most brilliant European avant-garde literatures of the twentieth century."[2] Drama critics first called the play a work of revolutionary importance surpassing in freshness and design the three productions Mihura had staged several years before. They expressed astonishment upon learning that a comedy of such neoteric sincerity could have been written a full twenty years and fourteen days before its première. Surprisingly, many of them declared the play was still before its time. Even as late as 1959, Jorge Collar, writing for *La Estafa Literaria,* averred that the play's only defect lay in the fact that it was still too modern.[3]

Immediately following the play's performance in Paris, some six years after its appearance on the Spanish stage, French reviewers accorded the work a similar recognition as an avant-garde production, noting that in its manuscript form, Mihura's play was a forerunner in spirit to the provocative absurdist theater of Ionesco. Writing for *Dimanche-Presse,* one critic extolled the terrible melancholy lying beneath its surface humor and concluded that the play was an extraordinary comedy, a masterpiece of the modern theater.[4] Eugène Ionesco himself, often abrasive in his judgment of contemporary writers, recognized the literary and intellectual excellence of the work and maintained that its irrational style could invigorate the contradictions, the stupidity, and the absurdity of the human spirit far better than any argument of formal rationalism or mechanical dialectics.[5]

For twenty years following its composition, *Three Top Hats* was "that comedy that no one understood," a work so inimitable, so surprisingly original, that, as Mihura states, it "not only upset the spectators, but sowed terror in the hearts of those who read it."[6] Accordingly, commercial theaters would not touch the play; promoters dared not risk their money on it; and many of Mihura's close friends viewed the work with suspicion and advised him to shelve it away for a more opportune moment.

It was generally conceded that public taste was to blame for the play's long suppression. Yet even with the public's mellowing — refined, perhaps, by the impact and aesthetics of Mihura's previous plays and the disarming humor of *La Codorniz* — the unproduced play was still rejected by professional promoters and might never have been staged were it not for the work of a director named Gustavo Pérez Puig and two dozen University of Madrid students. *Three Top Hats* was finally premiered by the Teatro Español Universitario, an amateur group, in the state-subsidized Teatro Español on the night of November 24, 1952. There was only one performance, yet that single staging brought immediate repercussions, and opened the doors of the commercial theaters. As Emilio Aragonés wrote in 1963: "At last the clever impresarios understood something that neither they nor the vocational groups had understood before 1936: that Mihura's humor and their business interests were not antagonistic elements."[7] Within a few month's time, *Three Top Hats* was awarded the National Drama Prize as the outstanding play of the 1953 season. Public and critical favor was unanimous; the play's acceptance was universal. *"Three Top Hats,"* exclaimed José Monleón, "will remain in the history of the Spanish theater as one of the best works of our time."[8]

I   *Synopsis*

The play opens with the arrival of a young man named Dionisio to a second-class provincial hotel where he intends to spend his final night of freedom before marrying and settling down into the dreary domestic life of a conservative family. Suddenly, and for the space of that one night, Dionisio's world is turned upside down. His room is invaded by an unbelievable assortment of circus characters who, upon seeing the three top hats that Dionisio is trying on in order to decide which one he will wear to the ceremony, assume him to be a performer in a juggling act. Dionisio is willingly caught up in this fantastic atmosphere, pleased to welcome the unreality of a circus charade to help him forget the normal life that awaits him. In the midst of his adventure, Dionisio meets and falls in love with a beautiful young girl named Paula. She is a vivacious dancer, part of the strange troupe of actors staying in the same hotel. In the course of their one-night relationship, Dionisio discovers an inspiring magic in illusion, a temporary respite in a world of absurd fantasy, and he yearns to escape forever the dull life that his imminent marriage represents. In the end, however, Paula returns to the chiaroscuro of her own sad and gay life of the music hall, while Dionisio carries a fleeting taste of freedom back to his conventional world of propriety and boredom.

Clearly, no brief synopsis can capture the greatness of this unusual play. A common approach to an understanding of its literary value has been to point out its avant-garde features of language and stage action. While eminent drama critics and literary historians frequently mention the dislocated dialogue, the irrational rupture of logical replies, and the elements of the absurd in human behavior contained within the play, this approach, soundly supported by able scholarship, only acquaints the student of modern Spanish theater with the general tone and tenor of the work. It does not fully explain the poignant charm in the design and substance of the play. Were it to be judged only on its absurdist elements, *Three Top Hats* might well be classified, by comparison, as second in importance to Mihura and Tono's outstanding farce, *Neither Poor nor Rich,* or at best on a par with the equally absurd and compelling drama by Mihura and Calvo-Sotelo, *Long Live the Impossible.*

II *Interpretation and Analysis*

This comedy's superiority is based on a dimension of meaning that lies beyond the factors most commonly cited in connection with its avant-garde character. *Three Top Hats* is unlike any other Spanish play of its time. It combines an intellectual humor with a warm and convincing sense of humanity. The humor is sustained by unrealistic dialogue and by absurd action, while the vigorous sparkle of human tenderness in the substructure of the play is born of superb characterizations and upheld by an indefinable lyric element that generates credible spontaneity in an incredible atmosphere. In this one play, observed Adolfo Prego, "are contained all of the elements that Mihura will go on developing in his later comedies."[9] This is an important statement, for if indeed one may find in *Three Top Hats* a compressed intimation of the author's later creativity, then our appreciation for Mihura's first and best play will be greatly enhanced, knowing that with its conception a personal style is born, a style that gains meaning and eloquence in future works.

Perhaps the sophisticated dialogue will become dated and stale in the course of time. Mihura believes it already has. "The type of humor that *Three Top Hats* represents no longer holds interest," he stated in a recent interview.[10] Other published statements by Mihura indicate that the author clearly values his later plays over *Three Top Hats;* he considers the famous production of his youthful pen to have been "a mere experiment." Yet despite Mihura's personal bias, the play continues to be acclaimed his greatest endeavor, and its dialogue is upheld as an example of living, natural, expressive language.

A new and ridiculous use of familiar clichés produces the humorous impact. Common expressions undergo a process of dislocation, revealing human needs and evoking charitable laughter over human follies. This characteristic has been referred to as the happy blend of *piruetas* (the hilarious absurdities of dehumanization), with *punzadas tristes* (doses of sadness), "known by the catch in the throat and the tear in the eye."[11] This may be what one critic has in mind when he writes that Mihura "succeeds in passing off his contraband goods between laughter and foolishness."[12] Ionesco expresses the same idea in situating *Three Top Hats* between the world of Charlie Chaplin and that of the Marx Brothers.[13]

Judging from the above statements, one may conclude that the humor of *Three Top Hats* occupies a unique intermediate stage between tragedy and comedy, borrowing equally from sensations of heartbreak and *gracia* (lighthearted wit), suffering and playfulness, derision and veneration, as the pendulum of authentic human experience shifts in constant motion from one pole to the other.

Fernández Cuenca compares this oscillating medium of humor to the blurring action of a camera lens; deliberately placed before the true shape of things, it distorts the vision of reality, thus forcing the imagination to juxtapose dissimilar objects in search of an apparent logic.[14] The sum and substance of this explanation suggests that *Three Top Hats* approximates in general the concept of surrealism. It is in this connection that Juan Guerrero Zamora identifies Mihura as the inaugurator of a new style of humor in Spanish dramatic literature, a style based on the systematic rupture of commonplace notions in both form and content, designed to reveal "the fatuous, ridiculous, illusory, childish and, at the same time, tender substratum of our existence."[15] This "new style" is nonetheless very much the old *Codorniz*-style humor, where verbal distortions of logic promote a surrealistic climate.

The speeches of the saintly Don Rosario, the hotel proprietor who attends to Dionisio's lodging comfort, are a good example of this trait. Rosario, whose very name connotes a spirit of beatific kindliness and adoration, in keeping with his affable personality,[16] speaks in a gentle, soothing manner, but what he says tends to transgress laws of syntactical proportion and common sense. He employs what Guerrero Zamora terms "visionary hyperbole,"[17] an attribute of speech he shares in common with Dionisio. Occasionally their conversation contains a lack of logic approaching the absurd, while on other occasions the comedy resulting from a distortion of logical causality approximates the kind of "sick joke" or "black humor" that gained popularity in the Western world about a decade after the play's première. This is similar, in fact, to Mihura's former writings for *La Codorniz,* wherein verbal sallies represent an attempt at a superior, sophisticated attitude toward serious matters.

A common form of dislocated dialogue is the unlikely response to a simple question or a follow-up comment that thoroughly disarms the listener by its absolute irrelevance to the subject. This is the same practice noted in Mihura and Tono's *Neither Poor nor Rich.* Evaristo Acevedo characterizes this kind of humor as "preferentially non-temporal and abstract, with a thematic line directed against clichés, against linguistic commonplaces; . . . it follows a preconceived attitude of 'escape from reality'."[18] In addition to the projection of absurd notions through dialogue, Mihura also introduces elements in the action to advance the bizarre humor. Dionisio's struggle with a flea and his antics with the telephone in Act One are the two most notable examples.

Finally, the strange onstage proliferation of diverse physical objects contributes to the absurdity of the climate. Act One prepares the spectator for the gradual increase of unusual things, beginning with Dionisio's black satin pajamas with a white bird embroidered on the chest and Don Rosario's discovery of a man's boot under the bed. As the peculiar objects make their appearance, none is forgotten or discarded; they remain on stage and are utilized by various characters throughout the course of action. The man's boot, for instance, is used by Dionisio to strike a match later in Act One. Unlike the rapid multiplication of articles in Ionesco's theater, these objects do not overwhelm the characters, nor do they dominate the action; their progressive articulation does, however, offer us a taste of the proliferation that characterizes such plays as *The Chairs* and *The New Tenant*.

Briefly mentioned, the curious items in *Three Top Hats* include packages, bottles, coats, hats, musical instruments, tin cans, paper, medals, four dead rabbits, and four live dogs (concerning which Mihura adds "it would be marvelous to have them barking").[19] Add to this The Hateful Gentleman's gesture of removing from his pockets such articles as garters, stockings, a bouquet of flowers, a box of candy, two sandwiches, and a baby rattle, and one senses a clear resemblance between the action in this play and the spirit of a vaudeville act. This music hall climate is furthered by the presence of The Chorus of the Strange Old Men, who sing three popular songs in Act Two. To this atmosphere might be added the sound of music from a gramophone, frequent dancing about the stage, sudden entrances and hurried exits, the abrupt appearance of The Happy Explorer from beneath Dionisio's bed, and the equally surprising entrance of the Enamored Romantic from inside Dionisio's wardrobe.

It is no wonder that *Three Top Hats* shocked the sensibilities of many of Mihura's most liberal professional friends. Had it been permitted a première in 1932, it is possible that conservative theatergoers would have been brought to their feet, flustered, indignant, shouting. One promoter of that time, José Juan Cadenas, rejected the play on these very grounds: "It is so extraordinarily new in its form and method that if I were to stage it in my theater one of two things could happen: it would either be a tremendous success, or the public would set fire to the theater seats."[20] Manolo Collado's admonition to the playwright was as wise as it was inspired: "It is a play of such fine and unique humor that you must first prepare the public to understand what it's going to see."[21]

III *Characterization*

A warm and humane undercurrent, visible in all Mihura's comedies, is especially apparent in *Three Top Hats*. Here the author shows an unusual feeling and compassion for his fellow human beings. Though he deplores intolerance and stupidity, his portrayal of intolerant and stupid people is never personal or bitter. Even the reprehensible natures of Don Sacramento and The Hateful Gentleman are sympathetically drawn. This typically humane side of the author is a quality that in Spanish is called *ternura,* or tenderness, the word his critics use most frequently when writing about Mihura's plays. Other preferred adjectives, favored by critics and spectators alike, suggest the fact that soft emotions and lyric tones lend the playwright's comedies a value beyond that of sheer entertainment.

One unusual feature of *Three Top Hats* is that none of the *dramatis personae,* excepting Paula, conveys the impression of being an ordinary, typical, average human being. Yet all of them, including Paula, have a common naturalness. They are accurately drawn, although without profound psychological depth. Each undergoes a logical development despite Mihura's deliberate exaggeration for the sake of burlesque and caricature of the secondary figures. And they are wholly believable within the context of their intended roles. "In Mihura," observes Enrique Llovet, "there is never an absence of logic in the development of character."[22]

Dionisio, the young protagonist, is masterfully characterized through dialogue and action. Central to the plot and to the significance of the play is the stress Mihura places on his natural timidity and his excessive malleability. Though unsettled and shifting in his convictions, Dionisio is not deprecated as an abulic soul. He possesses, in fact, a profound desire to emancipate himself from the bondage of social conformity. He is a nonconformist in spirit and thus elicits an indulgent sympathy from the spectator who can

identify with Dionisio's suppressed wish for improvised adventure
and lasting freedom, but who senses his debilitating allegiance to
the degrading presumptions of the world. Dionisio is committed to
marry Margarita, a girl whose nature is "so vulgar that the author
... does not dare put her on stage through the entire play."[23] His
courtship has followed a standard pattern — seven years of solicita-
tion, the gradual acquiring of false illusions about happiness, and a
romance inspired by material considerations over love. His imminent wedding represents the final and inevitable consignment of his
mortal life to the dull, pedestrian order of habit.

Mihura points up the human weakness of his protagonist by presenting him in the sad and constant process of adopting the ideas of
others to form a part of his own susceptible personality. When
Dionisio shows his room to Paula, for instance, he acts toward her
just as Don Rosario had acted earlier toward him in showing him
the room. Paula expresses her notion that it is stupid to get married
and Dionisio agrees, thus contradicting his former belief. In the
same way, he accepts Don Sacramento's judgment about him,
namely, that he is a bohemian. This imitative personality trait in
Dionisio is also seen in the episode of the broken rattle. In Act Two
he plays with the toy while talking with Paula. It breaks and she repairs it for him. In Act Three the incident is repeated. But this time
it is Don Sacramento who breaks the toy and Dionisio who repairs
it.

Overall, Dionisio is so easily convinced, so readily influenced by
the opinions of others, that he is unable to master any situation.
His frantic fumbling with the telephone while Paula lies uncon-
scious on the floor is hilarious but illustrates also the tragic help-
lessness and confusion of Dionisio and how his weak character is
torn between conflicting allegiances. His struggle to seize an
alternative that could change his life for the better results in a negative choice. He rejects the personal liberation Paula represents for
him in favor of the puerile inertia which has thus far characterized
his vapid existence.

Dionisio enters the swift action of this play as an utterly bored
and boring individual. His life is suddenly infused with interest,
vitality, and charm, yet he voluntarily opts for the continuation of
insipid boredom. This is a common motif in Mihura's plays. We
have seen the theme of boredom operative in *Long Live the Impossible,* where Palmira's shift from a stuffy existence to the glam-

our of the circus milieu, then back again, is similar to Dionisio's escape from his true dull nature into the magic of the music hall world.

The same theme is also present in *The Case of the Slightly Murdered Woman,* which concludes with the total and absolute boredom of Lorenzo and Raquel after the stimulation of their successful murder of Mercedes. Boredom is the key message in *The Case of the Stupendous Lady* (*El caso de la señora estupenda*), a play in which a woman engages in the dangerous game of espionage in an effort to escape from a humdrum life, only to abandon the spy ring as ennui again overtakes her. Boredom as a motivating force weighs heavily upon *Three in Dim Light* (*A Media luz los tres*) and accounts for Sebastian's conduct and his basic failure with women. Boredom actuates Florita to enter a competitive man's world in *Sublime Decision* (*Sublime decisión*); it impels Juan to forsake a formal medical career for the spontaneous pleasures of a simple life in *My Beloved Juan* (*Mi adorado Juan*). Extreme boredom lies at the base of the frivolous and stupid lives of the adulterous couples in *Canasta* (*La canasta*), Mihura's greatest commercial failure and only unpublished play. Because of boredom Andrés visits Paris in *Ninette and a Gentleman from Murcia* (*Ninette y un señor de Murcia*), and the delightful satire surrounding Jerónimo and Mercedes in *Miracle at the López House* (*Milagro en caso de los López*) is precisely at the expense of their complete domestic boredom. To a lesser degree this theme is apparent in most of Mihura's other productions; it represents what Torrente Ballester terms his abiding "dislike and disgust for everything that smothers spontaneity."[24]

Returning to the character of Dionisio, we perceive that the melancholy which underlies *Three Top Hats* is partially due to the protagonist's inability to respond to the world of love and adventure, despite his enlightened view that such a world offers him the only true freedom. In terms of the protagonist's role, this is a play about the initiation of a young man into self-realization, and his resulting frustration upon finding himself bound to a rigid social mold and to the mediocrity of his own sorry existence.

The other aspect of the melancholic undercurrent in *Three Top Hats* is suggested by the character of Paula, who incarnates a profound human search for happiness. In contrast to Dionisio's passivity, Paula's life is characterized by motion. While Mihura offers no physical description of the girl other than to mention that

she is "a marvelous blond girl of eighteen years of age," we know
by her energetic pace, her quick replies, and her unstudied candor
that she represents a young person filled with a boundless joy of
living. She cares nothing for social rank, marriage, or responsi-
bility. Her pleasures are the innocent joys of infancy, like eating
crabs at the beach and building castles in the sand. She openly
rebels against any domineering force imposed on her life, as exem-
plified by her unwillingness to heed the dictates of her black manager and obvious lover, Buby Barton. She is a woman who allows
her emotions free rein and her vitality full expression. A product of
the music hall, Paula is the complete opposite of Dionisio's fiancée.
She is, in point of fact, a show-girl prostitute who, under the direction of her unscrupulous manager, exploits with her wiles and
feigned affections the wealthy strangers she meets.

Yet in her encounter with Dionisio, Paula suddenly wavers in her
self-sufficiency, approaching for a fleeting moment the sensation
of genuine love. What is remarkable about her contact with this
emotion is that Mihura does not permit her to enjoy the experience
as a whim, or to hold on to it sentimentally. Her final toss of the
three top hats at the close of the play signifies that she, too, will return to the norms and conventions of her own world, and her life
will go on as before. Paula's appearance, incidentally, like Maribel's in *Maribel and the Strange Family* (*Maribel y la extraña
familia*), is funny and surprising because the author has been preparing us to visualize a chaste Margarita; early allusions to Margarita's saintliness, purity, and virtue make Paula all the more
interesting to the spectator, as her professional interests become
manifest. The contrast between Paula and Margarita remains implicit throughout the play, for although Margarita never appears,
the kind of life she represents for Dionisio is clearly defined.

IV   *Mihura as Humanist*

The freedom that Dionisio and Paula discover is promptly anni-
hilated by the repressions and taboos of conventionalism. The
forces brought to bear against their rebellion emerge from the
stratified and dogmatic codes for human conduct symbolized in the
appearance of Don Sacramento, Dionisio's future father-in-law.
As his very name suggests, Don Sacramento represents the strict
and binding covenant that governs an obedient slave to decency. He

opposes improvisation of any kind and censures the mere appearance of deviation from prescribed patterns of human conduct. Ricardo Domenech calls him the symbol of unflinching puritanism, "the rigidity of pre-established, implacable habits, of which he is both slave and defender."[25] His inflexible system of morality is based on appearances and decent behavior. Whatever runs counter to these frozen standards is declared "bohemian," the same criterion employed by Don Vicente in *Long Live the Impossible* and by the antagonist Manríquez in *My beloved Juan (Mi adorado Juan)*.

Because Don Sacramento stands for the ridiculous mechanization of habit in human relations, Mihura depicts him with burlesque exaggeration. Don Sacramento is a complete caricature of mortal inanity, a smug and pompous individual whose ludicrous, even absurd, ideas leave no doubt concerning what facet of life he typifies. His brief appearance on stage in Act Three is unforgettable. Sputtering confused and excited exclamations about his daughter, he proceeds to define the norms of propriety that must govern the actions of all "decent persons." These include, among other things, hanging family portraits and chromolithographs on the walls, awakening every morning at six-fifteen, eating fried eggs for breakfast, chatting and playing dominoes with a semi-toothless old man on Sunday nights, and, when in the proper mood, taking two nights out a week for a wild spree on the town, "because the spirit also needs expanding."[26]

This is the same kind of humdrum, familiar existence that Don Sabino rebels against in *Long Live the Impossible,* the only difference being that in *Three Top Hats* banality is associated with the aristocracy, while the tedium of Sabino's world is middle class. This difference in class distinction is significant for, as we see reiterated in Mihura's later plays, the author's critical attitude toward intolerance and heartlessness is not confined to a particular social level, but is directed at human stupidity in any rank or station.

Don Sacramento's advice to Dionisio contains a delightful admixture of topical and poetic expressions. One of his utterances recalls Rubén Darío's *Sonatina:* "The child is sad. The child is sad and the child weeps. The child is pale. Why do you torment my poor child?"[27] He repeats these words several times. His short, exclamatory sentences produce the effect of a broken phonograph record or the prefabricated speech of a mechanical man. The intentional rephrasing of a familiar verse contributes to the overall depiction of Don Sacramento as a thoroughly unoriginal person, one who, like Margarita in *Neither Poor nor Rich,* must depend upon the commonplace as the only avenue for forging a prescribed pattern of existence. Guerrero Zamora calls attention to the fact that Mihura's visible symbol for fatuity in this play — Don Sacramento's fried eggs — foreshadows Ionesco's emblem for the dullness of the unimaginative intellect — fried potatoes with bacon.[28] Indeed, one perceives in the caricature of Don Sacramento a resemblance to the grotesque mannikins who later make their appearance in the exciting and original theater of the absurd.

A great deal like Don Sacramento is the hateful old man whose lustful eye and financial eminence qualify him as another type to be caricatured with relish. The Hateful Gentleman incarnates incurable presumptuousness born of material wealth. Torrente, touching briefly on his importance to the play, makes the following valid comment: "He . . . is a perfect imbecile, whose life has crystallized into set and invariable forms. . . . Like Dionisio's future and inevitable father-in-law, he is made of pasteboard."[29] The Hateful Gentleman's *raison d'être* is reducible to money and sex. Domenech calls him "an erotic capitalist."[30] He determines to use his money for new conquests, paying no heed to his reputation. Mihura brings out the fact that he is a married man, thus making his reprehensible libertinism the antithesis of Don Sacramento's frozen morality, yet both men represent aspects of the same corrupt society; on the one hand, leaden conventions that canker the mind, on the other, graceless turpitude that debases the spirit.

Mihura's characteristic pose is one of detachment from ethical questions, but in this play he reveals himself a moralist. Through his deliberate caricature of Don Sacramento and The Hateful Gentleman, he becomes a spokesman for individual freedom tempered with good judgment and kindness as opposed to conformity to habits that shackle the spontaneous spirit. He contrasts the wanton license of The Hateful Gentleman with the childlike candor of Paula, thus establishing that rebellion and nonconformity become odious when defiled by anarchy, but are worthy of emulation when refined by seraphic joy.

It is this seraphic element in the heart of the play that lends the work its particular charm and dignity. And no character functions better to establish this tone of chaste innocence than the angelic

Don Rosario, the eccentric proprietor of the hotel in which all of the nonsense and the enchantment of one night occur. Don Rosario lends symmetry to a night of apparent chaos. He has the first and the last lines in the play, the one a greeting, the other a farewell. His solicitous care for Dionisio throughout the long opening scene of Act One establishes an atmosphere of delicate tone and provides visible demonstration of his generous affection and tenderness. His kindly speech infuses the scene with a magical dimension, preparing the spectator for the dreamlike transition into the surrealistic world of Act Two. This transition is softly and subtly realized toward the end of the first act when Don Rosario reappears to play a romance on his cornet in an effort to lull Dionisio to sleep. While he plays, absorbed in his art, a current of activity takes place on stage, as Fanny, The Hateful Gentleman, and Madame Olga enter, speak, and exit without the old man detecting their presence. This aura of tenderness is reaffirmed at the close of the play with Don Rosario's third and final appearance. He now transports us back to the inevitable reality of Dionisio's commitment, effected in a beatific climate of love and flowers.

Rosario's speech and manners betoken a disposition of untroubled innocence. Yet his is an anachronistic nature. His generation — marked by unselfish service and consideration for others — is contrasted to a rising generation of exploiters like Buby Barton and his carnival troupe, whom Don Rosario disparages with the words, "they are very bad and they mess up everything," and whom Don Sacramento censures as part of an age of "great European swindlers and international vampires."[31] Dionisio reminds Don Rosario that his generosity is overdone and that his guests take undue advantage of him. Rosario's continual improvements to the hotel without an increase in rates will bring him to financial ruin, Dionisio observes. But Don Rosario is only concerned about the physical comforts of his guests, whom he treats with inordinate paternal love, as though they were his own children.

The old man's charm is also conveyed through his frequent use of romantic, botanical epithets for Dionisio, such as "little face of nard," "little cocoon of gilliflower," "honeysuckle face," as well as his sentimental interest in Dionisio's impending marriage. His faulty vision, long white beard, rotundity, and nostalgic attachment for his old hotel contribute to the endearment he imparts. Rosario is very much a forerunner of Doña Vicenta and Doña

Matilde, those sweet, eccentric, and winsome old ladies in Mihura's later stage success, *Maribel and the Strange Family* (*Maribel y la extraña familia*).

The exceptional group of people who comprise the carousel climate of Act Two warrants special attention. They include actors and dancers, members of a theatrical troupe on tour through the Spanish provinces; residents of the seaside resort town where the play's action takes place; and miscellaneous bearded revelers of international stock. According to Mihura's statement, they form "an absurd and extraordinary chorus."[32] Their actions are characterized by unrestraint, pretense, and foppery. Instant joy is first on their agenda, and in their eagerness to magnify an unbridled vitality, they imbue the amoral atmosphere of Dionisio's bedroom with exotic and erotic tones.

Thematically they function as a radical contrast to the placid monotony of Dionisio's world, so severing his blind devotion to a false ideal. For it is through Dionisio's brief contact with this "hippie" element that he comes to detest the notion of stringent uniformity in thought and in conduct; through his brief acquaintance with Paula he comes to realize how sad and ugly his fiancée really is, with her genial manners, her elegant dress, and her twelve facial moles. The magnetism of a permissive climate has shattered his faith in the supremacy of conventionalism.

Yet at the same time this informal world of Paula and her friends is a sham. Buby reminds Paula that scruples and emotions must be stifled, for the only reality of the music hall profession is the hard work necessary to deceive and exploit. The schematic and underdrawn secondary characters suggest the vague and superficial values that really lie beneath the plating of this free and indulgent milieu. With the exception of Paula, the members of the music hall retinue appear to be made. Each one is a caricature, displaying some facet of frivolity and irresponsibility. Their demeanor and gestures betray the hidden emptiness of their lives, the same kind of vacuity and senselessness that Palmira discovers in the circus world of *Long Live the Impossible*.

In a manner similar to the play just mentioned (written in collaboration with Calvo-Sotelo), the systematic skepticism of Miguel Mihura once again establishes a position of deliberate ambiguity. Neither Dionisio's world nor Paula's offers the proper solution. Rational clarifications are still wanting with the final toss of the three top hats, and the spectator is obliged to choose the order he or she prefers. This ambiguity, observes José Monleón, is important to the poetics of Mihura's theater, for the author reveals in this way "the absence of a logical order, thus demonstrating that facts are not univocally explicable."[33] Monleón points out that ambiguity becomes a positive value in Mihura's productions, for with it the playwright replaces the sentimental concept of the happy ending with a sense of true perspective, "making known the relativity of certain values and the necessity of freely facing the interpretation of situations."[34]

The two opposing worlds of *Three Top Hats* are, in reality, "essential states of the same society."[35] In this sense, their inevitable coexistence is justified, but when love issues forth from the interrelation of these two diametrically opposed concepts of life, the relationship, as Ricardo Domenech states, is "proscribed beforehand, a love condemned"[36] by forces stronger than either Dionisio and Paula. Mihura symbolizes this fact in the transfer of the dance hat from Paula to Dionisio, a hat too large and unbecoming for him; and Paula's playful tossing of Dionisio's three formal top hats in Acts One and Three. The dichotomy between the two worlds symbolized by the hats is also expressed by Buby as he says to Paula, "gentlemen love women like you, but they marry others."[37]

Throughout Mihura's theater there is an implicit critique and satire on the self-satisfied bourgeoisie and their materialistic attitudes. In *Three Top Hats* the criticism is incisive, directed largely at Don Sacramento. Yet even he, a caricature of the mechanized mind, is not denied some saving qualities as a human being; in his love for Margarita and his devotion to routine, we perceive a sympathetic side to his nature. While Mihura defends the free and unconventional life, he is unwilling to paint the world in terms of black and white. Subtle areas of grey are found in both camps, as we have noted in Dionisio's struggle to compromise with Paula's environment and Paula's attempts to link her world with his. For, after all, the basis of Mihura's concern is not morality, but rather humanity. It would be unfair to describe the author's dislike of artificial living without pointing to his interest in the positive worth of his charming characters and their personal struggle to gain freedom from artificiality.

Fundamental to *Three Top Hats* is a theme that Mihura has continued in many of his subsequent plays, namely, that everyone must find his or her own role in life. In Mihura's conception, this idea has no religious or philosophical background; he simply presents a problem central to the welfare of the individual himself. Dionisio's awakening reveals the high premium Mihura places on the value of a human being's choice. Dionisio may have made the wrong choice, but even in defeat his decision reaffirms the authentic meaning in Don Sabino's utterance from Act Three of *Long Live the Impossible,* that "happiness only resides in being what one has wanted to be."

Significantly, *Three Top Hats,* like the two former plays in Mihura's avant-garde production, lacks the optimistic view that love alone is a liberating force. Dionisio's desire to flee with Paula to London, Havana, or Chicago, is the result of his long-suppressed determination to break away from a narrow-minded reality in order to reach a larger freedom. Paula represents the catalyst that accelerates his doubts concerning the value of his intended as a future wife and companion. Yet love itself serves no real purpose in effecting a new direction. Dionisio fails, just as in *Long Live the Impossible* Palmira fails in giving up Fede to have economic security by marrying Vicente, or, as in *Neither Poor nor Rich,* Abelardo fails in his relationship with Margarita.

Love tends not to fulfillment but to fiasco in *Long Live the Impossible, Neither Poor nor Rich,* and *Three Top Hats.* Thematically, the negative importance of love sets these three plays apart as comprising a unique category in the playwriting of Miguel Mihura. Indeed, it is interesting to note that following his first productions, Mihura adopts an entirely different point of view; he later portrays love as a positive attribute leading to freedom and happiness. *The Case of the Slightly Murdered Woman* is the first example of this new posture. The play not only exalts love as a positive value but includes the more fashionable happy ending that becomes from this play forward a typical formula in Mihura's writings. The author's later optimistic view could well be a gesture to his audience, for Mihura was willing to compromise a great deal to public taste in an effort to increase his personal revenue.

Despite the playwright's enormous popularity and corresponding box-office success since the year 1952, not at any later date in his writings has he created a play so full of poetic meaning, so full of life as *Three Top Hats,* for Dionisio's confrontation may be seen as the most important crisis of the human experience. The world of play and fun and shining happiness that he senses in Paula's bohemian society occasions a personal conflict that is both touching and unforgettable. And it affords Miguel Mihura the opportunity to be a spokesman for compassion and tolerance, the ideals most fundamental to his personality and to his plays.

CHAPTER 6

Theater of Intrigue

FOR many years Mihura has been an assiduous reader of detective fiction. His bookcases contain volumes of Agatha Christie, Ronald Knox, Dickson Carr, William Irish, and Georges Simenon. Mysteries are practically the only type of literature Mihura now reads, and understandably the tantalizing world of mystery and suspense has permeated his own dramatic productivity. The detective figure, often an eccentric, error-prone caricature of Sherlock Holmes, appears in five plays, while the perpetration or intimation of a serious crime invades more than half of his theatrical writings. These are generally comedies of an exacting construction, and some among them are prodigious examples of the playwright's technical mastery. The observable constants in this genre are Mihura's devotion to the enigmatic qualities of the female protagonist, his effort to find endearing and enduring human sentiments in all characters, and his concern for the role of boredom in giving rise to or resulting from a major criminal act.

I *The Tale of a Neurotic Spy*

Boredom is a key message underlying both the action and the impact of *The Case of the Stupendous Lady* (*El caso de la señora estupenda;* 1953). The play, inspired by wartime events in Italy,[1] concerns the misadventures of a beautiful, self-serving international spy named Victoria Karlovich, whose initial plunge into espionage is motivated by her need to escape from a life of tedium. She ultimately abandons the spy ring because ennui again envelops her, once she grows accustomed to the humdrum sameness of constant danger. The other characters are also the begetters and victims of their own stale existence. They gyrate and chatter in a paroxysm of self-induced world-weary discomforts. Their insipid exchanges and silly engagement in the reversals of spy-duping bathes the reader or audience with wearisome banalities. This light farce in three heavy acts is unworthy of comparison with Mihura's better plays.

Mihura confesses that he also is puzzled over the meaning of this commercially propelled comedy: "I haven't the least idea what it is all about."[2] Yet he manages to sustain our interest in its flimsy and quite aimless story line by virtue of a neatly measured dramatic construction. If craftsmanship can compensate for a prevailing lack of substance, some twelve of Mihura's plays, including *Stupendous Lady,* are commendable skeletal masterpieces; but if judged in terms of their plot coherence or depth and consistency of characterization, well over half of Mihura's production should be consigned to semi-oblivion. This may be what Monleón has in mind when he dismisses *Stupendous Lady,* among several of Mihura's plays of secondary importance, for its "radical falsity."[3]

The protagonist's quest for new excitement in her life begins, as does the play, on her wedding night. She — Victoria — has been taken into the foreign war zone of her groom's country for their honeymoon. Once established in their suite, many strange incidents occur, all of which function to remove any similarity to a typical wedding night. In the first place, Alejandro, the moody and bad-tempered husband, loses their marriage license. They are then obliged to share their room with a cynical dandy named Carlos, whom the maid mistakes for Victoria's husband. When Alejandro's former fiancée arrives, a girl of extreme stupidity named Susana, the stage is set for a long series of semi-absurd confrontations involving Alejandro's rage, Susana's jealousy, Victoria's disgust, and Carlos' despicable egotism.

Victoria is on the verge of sailing for Montevideo to get a divorce when a government inspector, suspecting that she is a foreign spy, forbids her departure. Alejandro too accuses her of traitorous espionage activities and declares an end to their one-day marriage of convenience. Things look bleak for Victoria, who had married simply to secure a passport and to escape from the tediousness of her dull existence. But playboy Carlos, who also suffers from a chronic case of boredom and moreover believes her innocent of any wrong-doing, intervenes. He phones his cousin the Minister to arrange a safe-conduct pass for Victoria. The minister's wife, as it happens, is an old-time friend of the hapless Victoria, and she knows that

Victoria is in truth a foreign spy. Nevertheless, the pass is granted in the name of friendship. Victoria then learns that the fact that she is a spy is no longer a threat in Alejandro's country; a new alliance has converted her from an enemy into an ally. She is now permitted to leave for Montevideo, but not without first spending a few pleasant moments with her new-found lover and protector, Carlos. They exchange pleasantries while bombs whistle and explode about them. As the play ends, Victoria is seen to be vacillating between the notion of staying on with Carlos until boredom drives them both apart and the idea of departing for South America to search for a different kind of existence, likewise filled with tedium.

One major difficulty in *The Stupendous Lady* is its immoderately pessimistic tone. There is not a truly likeable individual in the entire cast. Victoria, for instance, pursues her own self-interest without regard or respect for the feelings of others. Some of her ostensibly fine qualities — a dash of surface poise and a flare for self-assurance — are merely masked mannerisms hiding her basic cynical distrust of people. Her actions constantly belie her honeyed words. She hinders everyone's chances for happiness by her own selfish quest for diversion and is herself unhappy and insecure. The play's title is ironic, for this "heroine," who gives every appearance of becoming a self-possessed and liberated woman, falls far short of being "stupendous." Her "case" remains an unresolved clinical study of a pathologically neurotic female.

Nor is her false married partner any better. Alejandro's quick temper, his inconstancy with women, his inane behavior in the presence of both his wife and his former fiancée, and his ill-conceived sense of timing bring him before us as a most unlovable fool. Carlos is even worse. He is nothing but a hypocritical, moneyed parasite, always ready to find new diversions at the expense of other's hopes and dreams. Susana is perhaps the least impressive personality of the lot. Her limited mentality makes her a simple annoyance to the other characters as well as to the audience. Perhaps the lacerating severity of Mihura's farcical pessimism dislodges the comic potential of this witless woman; she shifts from her function as a jealous ninny toward a silly caricature of herself, appearing more an embarrassment to the script than a contributing factor in its denouement.

It might be argued, of course, and to Mihura's credit, that his assembly of negative and farcical creatures in *The Stupendous*

Lady is a deliberate portrayal of the loss of vital human dimensions in the face of wartime peril. Truly, everyone in the play has been shattered by the armed conflict, and the nonsense displayed in their conduct and dialogue may well be interpreted as a logical consequence of abnormal social conditions. Yet this is no protest play: Mihura offers no earnest social commentary, develops no political or moral thesis, and leaves his audience no reason for taking sides. While there is a strong mocking tone throughout the play, Mihura aims his only criticism at certain negative aspects of human nature. He limits any overt social reproach to the obvious revelation of his characters' concern for appearances and to a facetious gibe on the widespread evil of bureaucratic nepotism.

Had Mihura not endowed his characters with more than their share of frivolous mentality, or had he related their mindless behavior more realistically to the milieu that bred them, he might have produced a play of valid social importance and lasting literary value. But having once abandoned his promising avant-garde or "revolutionary" pose, clearly evident in three of the plays before 1950, Mihura was not to show further signs of such a stance. His theater would now be known as a vehicle for mass entertainment, a model of tender and humane characterizations, a noncommitted, relaxed art of compromise to public taste, a craft for the perpetuation of easy laughter in the contemporary mold of Spanish humor.

II   *A Piece in Dead Earnest*

Intended first as a script for cinematography,[4] *A No-Account Woman* (*Una mujer cualquiera*) was written during a period when Mihura was outspoken in his dislike for the legitimate stage. He had experienced severe financial reversals in the production of his three plays of collaboration with Tono, Calvo-Sotelo, and Laiglesia and thus turned to movie script writing to improve his material well-being. When, five years later, the script was rewritten for the theater, it remained brutally faithful to cinematographic realism, complete with stark, metallic dialogue, a protracted rash of episodic scenes, percolating with melodramatic intensity, and a low literary tone. Resembling neither Mihura's earlier or later writings, the plot of *A No-Account Woman* edges toward that brand of serious drama associated with the tragic narratives of internationally known mystery writers. Violence and cruelty replace the characteristic Mihurian moods of human tenderness and gentle satire. A grim moral thesis stalks the protagonist in her lonely search for understanding and love, and an authentic criminal phere envelops the schematic movement of events.

The play begins with the enactment of a carefully planned murder. Nieves, who perceives herself as a weak and worthless woman of the streets, is led by the treacherous Antonio to a chalet on the outskirts of Madrid. There she becomes the intended witness to a premeditated killing and is subsequently abandoned by her escort to answer for the crime he has just committed. Confused and frightered, Nieves flees the scene of the crime, only to be pursued by the police, who have discovered several clues that Antonio left behind to implicate her. Desperate to talk over her plight with a friend, Nieves turns to Rosa, a former companion from a more wanton past. Rosa does not provide the needed encouragement, but deeply shames and wounds Nieves with her reproaches. Having repudiated her profligate ways, Rosa is now concerned about protecting a "respectable" young man from the likes of Nieves; she is engaged to a fine man named Luis who, as it turns out, is none other than the murderous Antonio.

A dramatic encounter between Nieves and Antonio (Luis) cannot be avoided. Nieves' dependent and trusting nature makes her an easy prey for Antonio's magnetic dominance. She believes she will be secure and happy living with him, but for his part, Antonio plans to delude her again by building a stronger case to prove his innocence and to assure her involvement in the previous crime. She neither suspects that Antonio detests her nor that the police already know she is innocent. Her self-doubt and feelings of guilt over a crime she did not commit add a piteous dimension to her already pathetic character.

In the final act Nieves discovers that Antonio is preparing to flee. He has planted the murder weapon in her coat as a final piece of incriminating evidence. Unable to believe his betrayal, she clings to the illusion that his promises of love are sincere. Antonio is a heartless villain; he mocks her debilitating dependency and degrades her sense of allegiance to him. This unbearable deception drives her to destroy Antonio: she shoots him with the same gun he had placed in her coat pocket. As a final touch of melodramatic irony, Antonio's death coincides with the moment in which the police have exonerated Nieves from the original crime. The protagonist's drastic act of vengeance is a logical consequence of her desperate state of mind. The assassination of Antonio is her only forceful act of rebellion against the man who had betrayed her, the society that had made her a harlot, and the frailty of her own character.

Unfortunately, though, cheap suspense reigns over psychological depth. While Nieves is believable, her sentimental conflict over Antonio is weakened by histrionics. Her personality cries out for greater development, but Mihura prefers to hand us the shouts and whimpers of an emotionally distraught woman superficially examined. As an emotive force for entertainment, *A No-Account Woman* is superb. In this respect alone, Luis Molero, writing for Madrid's *La Estafeta Literaria,* considers it one of Mihura's best plays.[5] But lacking as it does any provocative penetration as a character study, and failing also to provide the kind of poetic tension that could reveal more fully the pervasiveness of Nieves' alienation and thereby offset the playwright's excessive artifice and intrigue, the play, as a work of literature, is incomplete and disappointing.

III *The Mystery Play of Faultless Construction*

Carlota is the best of Mihura's detective thrillers and is technically an exceptionally fine play. His film experience enabled him to create an intricate, carefully designed series of flashbacks, often one within another, in which the planting of false clues, deceptive motives, and fresh suspicions delay until the final dramatic scene the unraveling of the mystery. The principle victim is the protagonist herself, Carlota, whose clever and calculating nature is so ably delineated that the audience is never quite certain of her next move. Believing that her first spouse died of boredom and fearing that she will also lose Charles Barrington, her current husband, because she lacks a certain spark of vitality in her character, Carlota contrives to excite Charlie by clouding her personality with an air of enigma. She makes him believe she is a murderess, a scheming specialist in the use of deadly poisons. But then, as one character's mysterious death follows another and strange happenings seem to corroborate the tales she launches to support her charade, both the audience and Charlie begin to fear for his life. So possessed with terror is Charlie that he decides to destroy his wife before she succeeds in eliminating him also.

The main course of the action traces the gradual conversion of Charlie's affection for Carlota into dread. In the space of one year's time her captivating lie thoroughly demoralizes and terrifies him. For her part, she is so caught up in the deception, so concerned that Charlie's interest in her will diminish if she ceases the charade, that she soon involves her friends in the conspiracy. When they too become mysteriously ill and accuse Carlota of having poisoned them, the exciting joke suddenly takes a turn toward the macabre. Other coincidental deaths among her acquaintances finally convince Charlie that he must take action, and as a result of her excessive zeal to stimulate Charlie, Carlota meets a violent end at the hands of an insecure and intimidated husband.

Though his act of murder is carefully planned, Charlie fails to protect his alibi. One of Carlota's friends, a flighty hypochondriac with whom Charlie is in love, implicates him shortly after he has learned to his grief that Carlota was not a murderess and that all of her alleged crimes were an invention to tantalize his imagination and keep their marriage interesting.

Carlota offers minimal situational comedy, except insofar as the play's foreign atmosphere — the setting is London in the year 1907 — would naturally amuse a Spanish audience. A general current of amusement derives from Mihura's intricate weaving of suspicion around certain characters and his later surprise twists to eliminate that suspicion; but overall this impeccably constructed drama preserves the difficult balance between serious and lighthearted comedy, leaning to the side of sobriety. The element of suspense is ever present; Mihura leaves his audience unaware of the solution until the very end. He uses a large retinue of secondary characters to increase the aura of mystery. They play out their roles in all seriousness, but the pseudo-serious circumstances of their interaction suggest that the playwright's aim may have been to parody the typical British murder drama in vogue at the time the play was premiered.

Spanish critics greeted *Carlota* as superior to the mysteries of Agatha Christie. Its decisive action and tightly-woven plot, carried to mathematical exactness, accord the work a singular importance among Spanish thrillers.[6] "Everything in the play is measured, tested, fitted to a perfect theatrical line.... The solution to the complications has been tackled with the greatest care, sharpness, ... and verisimilitude."[7] Ruth Richardson declared that its "tremendous success . . . reaffirmed Mihura's position among the great writers of the universal contemporary theater."[8]

The mechanical solidity of *Carlota* is praiseworthy, but still another element deserving commendation for special literary value is the precise psychological depth of Carlota's role. At no time is her character subordinate to the action. Unlike Hilton, the investigator from Scotland Yard whose mildly deformed and farcical conduct satirizes the intrepid and overzealous British sleuth, and unlike Charlie Barrington, whose feeble personality is equal to the weakness of his development as a character, Carlota is a strong and convincing heroine whose playful nature hides a brooding insecurity and on many occasions manifests a human sensitivity rivaling the best of Mihura's female protagonists.

The continuous retrospection in *Carlota* is fatiguing, though consistent with Mihura's cinematographic technique. Constant flashbacks function to preserve suspense, deepen the intrigue, and surprise the audience; but they compel every spectator to exercise a high level of concentration throughout the lengthy production. Like Jardiel Poncela's dazzling comedy, *Heloise Lies Under an Almond Tree,* Mihura's play is infused with isolated complications and mischievous subplots. But in contrast to Jardiel's hilarious theatrical madness, Mihura maintains a temperate and sober tone.

IV   *The Saccharine Nun as Sleuth*

A nun who becomes involved with a band of robbers embodies the farce and intrigue of Mihura's fourth mystery play, *Peaches and Syrup (Melocotón en almíbar).* Sor María is a meddling and highly imaginative do-gooder who calmly disrupts the scheme of four nervous criminals by her haphazard observations and auspicious remarks. She enters a tenement to care for an aged member of the gang whose case of pneumonia has obliged the group to halt in mid-stream their criminal activities. Among the robbers is one unwilling participant named Nuria, a former cabaret dancer whose complicity has been secured by false promises of a quiet, secure life as Federico's wife. Federico is a brutal ex-waiter who threatens her with physical abuse unless she remains with the gang. The leader of the group, a neurotic and bickering young man named Carlos, deteriorates emotionally as his fears of apprehension increase. Nuria's characterization, while promising in the early stages of the play, remains undeveloped because Mihura converts her into a pitiable creature constantly intimidated by others and unable, therefore, to surmount the conditioned response of her submissive nature.

Only Sor María stands out as a strong and decisive character. One of Mihura's most unusual protagonists, she functions to unveil the mutual distrust the criminals harbor for one another and to set in motion the operation of a law of moral justice and retribution. Involved in a lone investigation, she innocently plants in the minds of each criminal a sense of desperate terror at being discovered. Yet one is never quite certain how much Sor María really knows. Most of her uncanny precognition is the result of extraordinary guesswork. Her active imagination often leads her dangerously near the truth, only to swerve off in the direction of a romantic interpretation of the facts or a blatantly false deduction. Her suspicions and persistent verbal needling so upset the gangsters that they flee, leaving their stolen jewels behind. Of greater significance to the moral implications behind this comic demonstration that crime does not pay is the clear "lesson" Mihura conveys that each crook has been made aware of the perils of dishonesty for having known the irreproachable nun, Sor María.

The playwright's able management of Sor María's role holds the play intact. Her jocose innocence, reminiscent of Chesterton's Father Brown, contrasts brilliantly with the tortured fears of her antagonists, thus establishing a comical line of antithesis and reversal that runs as a steady current of humor throughout the work. Mihura combines in this felicitous female figure the contrary attributes of casual lucidity and a daft naiveté. As a lamb among wolves, Sor María deploys faith-inducing counsel to mitigate Nuria's frantic despair and enable the more hard-core criminals to perceive their limitations and mortal sins. Her serene nature opposes the gangsters' volatile nervousness, while her frequent use of saccharine diminutives and syrupy phrases among those who revel in coarseness adds a further dimension of contrast to a humor founded on contraposition of motive, speech, and action. One common critical response to the play is that it consists too much of one character: "the entire farce is Sor María with her revelations." Mihura's preoccupation with a single personality "gives a certain heaviness to the play" and "limits the possibility of defining well the human dimensions of the other characters."[9]

V *Prosaic Trickery That Goes to Seed*

Mihura's productivity was unusual during the 1964–65 theater season. Within seven month's time he staged and personally directed three major plays, giving every indication that Don Miguel, that casual, lazy, even plodding writer, was suddenly imbued with Alfonso Paso-like fevers of fecundity. But it proved more a prelude to the playwright's swan song than an initiation of spirited activity. Over the next three years he returned to the routine schedule of measured quiescence, bent upon his coveted dream of definitive retirement.

Of the three plays produced during Mihura's only prolific season, two were so frivolous they tended to diminish rather than enhance their author's literary reputation. The first of these, *Miracle at the López House* (*Milagro en casa de los López*), begins with a modicum of promise but ends in a muddled swirl of deficiencies. Its opening action centers on the monotonous existence of Jerónimo and Mercedes López, who have spent their entire life confined to their chalet, arguing to dispel the terrible weight of boredom that has settled on their bland lives. When not engaged in a domestic spat, they fritter away their time watching television. Their days are patterned by routine, their marriage impaired by ennui, their ambitions throttled by the possession of too much money. Nothing has disturbed their isolation from and indifference toward the outside world. Their clothes are too old or too small because Jerónimo refuses to go shopping. Their car has not functioned in nine years because they won't take the trouble to have it repaired. Divorce is prohibited and separation is too much effort, while murder — a seemingly viable alternative to boredom in *Carlota* — is unthinkable because one's tedium would increase if living alone.

We learn in the course of Act Two that Jerónimo has deliberately concocted this life-style to avoid detection. His wealth is the result of a successful robbery committed shortly before he met Mercedes. Though unaware of his criminal past, Mercedes married him, not for love, but to escape the pathetic humdrum misery of her own dreadfully romantic life. Her docile and gullible nature made her well suited for Jerónimo's purposes, and it was not long before she succumbed to his entreaties for a reclusive existence.

Everything changes when Mercedes, tired of the dullness of their established routine, suggests that they take in guests. No sooner has she done so when a young woman named Elvira arrives, brought to the house by an "angelic" taxi driver who recommended the home to her as a good place of lodging. A few moments later a second guest calls at the door. He is Cristóbal, a strange young man who earns his living as a professional hypnotist, and whose presence terrifies Jerónimo with fears that his past crime will be discovered.

At this juncture the focal point in the comedy shifts from the López couple to the family maid, Teresa. Because of the unexpected arrival of two mysterious guests, Teresa is obliged to work on her night off. She is infuriated at this unforeseen turn of events, having intended that very night to accept the amorous favors of her boyfriend's rival. The "miracle" of the house guests works to her salvation, however, for she ultimately interprets the intrusion as a providential rescue from the temptation of a carnal act. Convinced that her relationship with her boyfriend will henceforth be a meaningful experience, Teresa believes with Mercedes that the taxi driver who brought Elvira must have been Teresa's Guardian Angel, possibly conjured up by Cristóbal's hypnotic powers. And so the play ends, gliding preposterously with loose strings on a sea of alleged magic, hallucination, and inane supernatural occurrences.

That Teresa finds happiness in a genuine human relationship may be a valid justification for all the hocus-pocus, but Mihura, from Act Two onward, systematically destroys the poetic atmosphere by explaining away all illusions. Had he permitted a dimension of magic and unreality to exist for its own sake or in an unexplained and illusive way for the sake of Teresa's renewal, the work might well occupy a singular place in his repertory and would equal some of Alejandro Casona's enchanting supernatural plays. Regrettably, though, Mihura reduces unreality to a prosaic concatenation of cheap stage tricks. In the final scene, for example, he introduces a golden angel flapping her silly wings behind the living room drapes. Earlier he renders rational explanations to every aspect of the enigma, as though duty-bound to disentangle the teasing complications in a classical whodunit. He does succeed in destroying winsome humor and distorting a felicitous and seductive strain of fantasy. The delicate atmosphere of an authentic balance between reality and appearance, so well sustained in Act One, gives way to pedestrian vacillation and a vulgar denouement in Acts Two and

Three, respectively. "The play," says Manuel Adrio, "changes into narrative. The spectator is no longer offered situations, he is fed explanations."[10] And it is by reiterative explanations that Mihura severs that rarefied identification he had first established between the audience and the stage, sacrificing fluid, subtle imagination for literal disclosures.

While Mihura labors to solve the riddles of the miracle, he fails to resolve the mystery underlying Elvira's past life, Cristóbal's uncertain presence, and Jerónimo's nervous guilt over his crime. Elvira's history is the most bothersome: she claims to have come to Madrid seeking the father of her illegitimate child. The play ends without revealing to us whether or not she is successful in this quest. As for Jerónimo, we do learn that Mercedes, yet unaware of any robbery, had paid off her husband's debt to a criminal partner, but the unexpiated crime itself and Jerónimo's troubled conscience are never alluded to again. In a word, *Miracle at the López House* was an inspired idea that perished for lack of artistic nourishment. Arcadio Baquero defined it well as the play that "could have been the most extraordinary of Mihura's works."[11]

VI *The "Whodunit" Without a Crime*

The Teapot (La tetera) is Mihura's second play of limited literary consequence staged during the 1964–65 season. Following by only one month the première of *Miracle at the López House,* this two-act mystery is a suspenseful "whodunit" without an overt crime. It abounds with that delightful flurry of tête-à-tête humor García Pavón calls "the verbal magic" of Mihurian situational comedy.[12] Weaving a spell of mystery surrounding the unlikely relationship between a handsome man and his uncomely wife, this tightly constructed work reveals the power that subtle suggestions can wield in transforming an apparently innocent matter into a sinister affair. We first encounter the protagonist, Juan Maldonado, falsely accused of a crime he did not commit. Once exonerated, he no longer cares for the swinging, carefree excitement of his bachelor days in Madrid, so he settles down to a drab and tasteless existence with the singularly fat and unattractive Julieta, his provincial wife. Juan had married Julieta because she is the complete antithesis of every woman he has courted. Indeed, he lost so many beautiful and talented prospects to other men, that he is now determined to live with the one person whose mental, emotional, and physical attributes will repel all other suitors.

After two years of marital dullness with Julieta, Juan still appears to be enjoying a blissful, albeit colorless, domestic experience. Doting constantly on his loyal spouse, whose ugliness is compounded by a sickly constitution and many unsavory tics, Juan has successfully laid aside the memories of his past life — the exciting entertainment and the alluring women of his youth. However, with an unexpected visit of two old friends from the capital, Juan is again reminded of those glamorous days. His guests find his devotion to Julieta inexplicable, especially in view of the presence of Alicia, his wife's gorgeous younger sister, a woman who makes no pretense of her fondness for Juan.

The idea of deceiving Julieta has never occurred to Juan. But now the subtle workings of public gossip and the pressures exerted unwittingly by his house guests, his in-laws, and neighborhood visitors, not to mention the more obtrusive declarations of Alicia, trigger new emotional responses in Juan's heart. While still maintaining a strong outward appearance of love for Julieta, Juan is beginning to consider the possibility of a romantic liaison with the enticing sister. When a gas stove nearly causes Julieta's death, Alicia reveals to Juan her secret desire that Julieta might die, thereby freeing Juan from the bondage of his dull marriage. Alicia's shameless flirtations are partly the result of her openly seductive nature, and partly of hopeless boredom since the accidental death of her fiancé, who was killed while hurrying to obtain a teapot. The fact that Juan's friends from Madrid have brought him a teapot as a gift establishes a firm point of reference for all of the principals to discuss their concern for untimely deaths and grim forebodings.

As the play moves quickly to its conclusion, Juan, now openly aware of Alicia's affection for him, is no longer the serene and happy man seen earlier. Julieta, no longer a comfort to him, has become a barrier to his coveted relationship with Alicia. As the final curtain slowly falls, we see Juan in limbo, the brooding victim of his own uneasy emotions, nervously scheming which course to follow in an atmosphere charged with many understated suggestions that he is likely to commit a heinous crime. This final scene returns us to the same situation with which the play began, when Juan, then innocent of any wrongdoing, was accused of a serious crime.

The Teapot bears a thematic resemblance to José Echegaray's play, *El gran Galeoto,* a nineteenth-century verse drama about the evil effects of frivolous gossip on a couple's marriage. But whereas in the Neo-Romantic's work of 1881 the ultimate calamity is both presaged and depicted with all the histrionic clamor of melodrama, Mihura's enigmatic treatment remains a low-key suspense of the mind where plot is subordinate to dialogue and verbal pleasantries overshadow painful incidents. The vital purpose behind Mihura's play rests in the winsome humor one gleans from his study of Juan's big city habits in contrast to Julieta's provincial mentality, and the comic possibilities evoked from a climate of banter fused with an atmosphere of mystery.

Only in the last scene does the play undergo a violent shift of tone — highly unusual in Mihura's theater and suggestive of an Antonin Artaud or Fernando Arrabal play — as his gentle comedy gives way to the chilling intimation of a cruel homicide. It is this "bitter and disquieting" turn which has led several critics to remark that the generally consistent light tone of *The Teapot* does not argue for an unresolved and disconcerting finale.[13] Nevertheless, the ending does provide a neat cyclical balance, permitting the audience to enjoy Mihura's carefully structured contrast between appearance (i.e., the alleged crime) and reality (i.e., the intended crime) within a framework of dramatic symmetry. One might also point to the playwright's delicate use of ridicule and the grotesque in his caricature of Julieta and her provincial setting to serve as a bittersweet prelude to the sudden reversal of mood in the denouement.[14]

While the playwright develops the relationship between the thick-set Julieta and her ex-gallant spouse with unmatched artistry, he relegates the remaining six characters to function almost as spectators. As is the case with *Peaches and Syrup,* the suspense comedy where the nun Sor María dominates the action, here too the central characters overpower all secondary roles, devitalizing their dramatic potential. To Mihura's credit, however, is the excellent character delineation he transmits through dialogue. "Mihura possesses," asserts one observer, "as does no other contemporary Spanish writer, the secret of a dialogue in which every reply, though surprising and unexpected, remains completely believable on the lips of the character who states it."[15] To this end, *The Teapot* is an exquisite example of Mihurian theatrical construction, though it lacks the depth and transcendence of his best plays.

VII   *The Scheming Predator*

In *The Decent Woman* (*La decente;* 1967), Mihura develops another plot based upon a scheming wife's endeavor to induce her lover to execute a murder. But unlike Alicia in *The Teapot*, who communicates her impulse for wrongdoing in a discreet and subtle way, Nuria, the female protagonist to whom Mihura's ironic title, *The Decent Woman*, refers, is a vengeful, calculating, and sadistic purveyor of lies, intrinsically hostile and blatantly disposed to evil. Without question, Nuria is the most wicked character in Mihura's repertory. Strongly opposed to any notion of infidelity, Nuria's pretended decency hides a loathsome nature. Like Ibsen's Hedda Gabler, she is a monster beneath an outward appearance of social respectability. Her first husband was a wealthy Irishman with a cruel and drunken disposition who ended up mysteriously drowned in his bathtub. Her current husband is a rich, deaf Romanian whom Nuria detests and hopes to eliminate in exchange for amourous favors from his would-be slayer. To each man who desires to be her lover, Nuria demands that first he dispatch the Romanian.

Her latest prospect in a long-term effort to liquidate her spouse is Roberto, a weak-willed ninny quite incapable of perpetrating such a heinous crime. Easily manipulated and made of the same pitifully malleable substance as Dionisio of *Three Top Hats* and Andrés of *Ninette*, Roberto is intimidated by Nuria's proposal and decides to leave town. However, when the Romanian is discovered with his head smashed in, Nuria incriminates Roberto and the young man is arrested. His alibi proves meaningless, since he claims to have been with a prostitute at the time of the homicide and when the girl is asked to identify him, she refuses to do so.

Things look rather grim for Roberto until a fresh suspect emerges. Roberto's elderly servant, María, earnestly solicitous over her master's desire to marry Nuria, had gone to the Romanian's apartment with the intent to kill him. Clearly misunderstanding Nuria's evil motives, María had simply wanted to help Roberto find happiness. The Romanian, though, was already dead when María arrived. He had been bludgeoned with a candelabra by the boyfriend of the same prostitute with whom Roberto had spent the night when the crime was committed. Thus Roberto has been a patsy in the real killer's hands, cleverly set up to be accused of the slaying. And Nuria, hoping to escape from her promise to marry Roberto, attempts to seal his fate by directing all suspicions his way. In the end both Roberto and María are exonerated, though each has been degraded by the venom of Nuria's hatred for men. As for the protagonist, she too is free, bent on a new quest for fresh prey.

Bordering whimsically on the edge of being a serious detective thriller, *The Decent Woman* is one of Mihura's most engaging psychological comedies. Nuria's intelligence and cunning both reveal and conceal facets of a human enigma: on the surface she carries out games of vengeance against her male companions, while within she is at odds with the fantasies and lies that underlie a yearning for understanding and love. Nuria's distrust of men is the obvious result of a loveless childhood and two wretched marriages; but her compulsion to maintain a reputation of untarnished virtue while forever devising new artifices and deceptions with which to destroy others — and thereby imperil her own happiness — defies an easy and transparent explanation. "The true nature of the woman escapes us completely," writes S. Samuel Trifilo.[16] Nuria is complicated, disturbed, and bewitching. The stupid and cowardly men in her life are powerless to deal with her. The values and norms of society are incapable of controlling or correcting her. The laws of the land fail to punish her. And the driving, malignant forces in her psyche cry out unreservedly for new victims to ravage.

Unlike most of the individuals in Mihura's other mystery plays, the principals in this drama achieve no liberating or redeeming attributes. Only María, the old servant, who would have murdered the Romanian had she arrived on time, acts out of a sense of deep affection for Roberto. Her devotion to him is constant to the end. The others live in a realm of total selfishness and self-deceit. Nuria remains "decent" by her own warped standards, while Roberto, confused by his own abulic nature, is but a pathetic simpleton. Even after Nuria humiliates and spurns him, he still pleads for her companionship. And the prostitute, victimized by her dependence on a jealous pimp, sinks lower toward degradation when she serves as an accomplice to the Romanian's murder. The motivating factors behind all human conduct in *The Decent Woman,* aside from María's self-sacrifice, are lust and revenge. To this end the play is similar in its pessimistic tone and its portrayal of negative human traits to the first of Mihura's comedies of intrigue written fifteen years earlier, *The Case of the Stupendous Lady.*

VIII   *The Playwright's Last Crowd-Pleaser*

José María de Quinto remarked that if one were to compose a "New Art of Writing Plays," based on Lope de Vega's dictum that success in dramaturgy is measured by the playwright's ability to gratify the masses, one could examine the construction of Mihura's recent comedies for the best modern examples.[17] Indeed, Miguel Mihura's last play, *Only Love and The Moon Bring Good Fortune* (*Sólo el amor y la luna traen fortuna*) is an outstanding illustration of a work designed solely to please, to set at ease, to promote genial comfort for the bourgeois consumer of superficial farce and gratuitous laughter. Reversing the cynical leaning he manifests in *The Decent Woman,* Mihura turns to a crowd-pleasing, lighthearted piece that teems with gaiety and optimism.

The protagonist is a rich, pompous, and temperamental concert pianist named Amancio de Lara, a man who superstitiously attributes his success to extraordinary acts of good fortune. His career suddenly goes sour, however, in the wake of an automobile accident from which he escapes unscathed but wherein several others are seriously injured because of his negligent driving. His concern for their survival is only to protect his own international reputation. Amancio's good luck seems to return, at least momentarily, after he replaces a sick nurse with a destitute but cheerful student nurse named Mariló. She is an impoverished orphan, engaged to an odious man who cannot afford to marry her. Despite an unpromising background, she exhibits a bright and optimistic attitude toward life. Her winsome disposition convinces Amancio that her continued presence in the household will foster the spread of special salubrious magic. Desperately worried that his luck will shatter if Mariló departs, Amancio assigns the girl countless menial tasks, showering her as well with useless gifts and insisting that she smile and sing and bubble over with joy. During the first week of her service, Mariló is not allowed to leave Amancio's apartment.

Suddenly another woman arrives. She is Maritza, Amancio's on-and-off-again mistress. It is not long before she discovers that her old lover is unconsciously troubled by the likely prospect of falling in love with his nurse. Maritza is a wealthy married woman who delights in extramarital affairs and generally cares nothing for the feelings of others. However, as her presence seems to bring Amancio bad luck, she analyzes his undercurrent of irritation with his nurse as signaling the slowly emerging proof of his genuine affection for the young girl. Concluding that her deteriorating relationship with the pianist is a terminal problem, Maritza walks out on him for the last time.

Mariló now discovers that she has been hired simply to serve as a good luck charm for her master. In anger, she upbraids Amancio for his shallow dependency on superstition in order to avoid the harsh blows that reality bestows. She helps him recognize that it is love, not luck, that brings meaning and order into his empty life, and the play ends on the happy note that the lonely, middle-aged pianist will now have more than Chopin to keep him company.

Mihura's sympathetic portrayal of Mariló is the most arresting feature of this superficial last comedy. The little student nurse, battered by life's adversities, intimidated by a repulsive boyfriend, and respected only as a talisman by her egocentric employer, has every right to be bitter and self-indulgent. Instead, she displays equanimity and hope. Her function in the play is to supplant the myth that mere chance operates to enrich human relationships with the moral lesson that a lasting companionship must be based on supportive understanding. However, it should be noted that Mihura not only delineates Mariló with an open and trusting nature, but he shackles his heroine as well in chains of servitude. He sketches a one-sided relationship insofar as Mariló relates to her master, reminiscent of Eliza Doolittle's dependency on Henry Higgins. An underling throughout the play, Mariló is defined in terms of her service to the male protagonist's more dominant personality. She is clearly not the liberated female that Maritza represents. Though selfish and hedonistic in her outlook, Maritza remains unfettered. By her refusal to indulge her lover's demanding whims, she emerges as the more admirable of the two women.

CHAPTER 7

Plays of Parody and Satire

A S he turned away from the revolutionary impetus of his early
plays toward the adoption of formulas more easily digested
by an undiscerning bourgeois public, Miguel Mihura engineered
humorous situations to delight and distract. He found that spectators would pay well to hear a continual cascade of clever,
meaningless utterances; that they would not pay to witness the
unraveling of a provocative, serious plot; that they preferred the
patent manners and conformist molds of parody, satire, and caricature to thoughtful human dramas. Mihura never relinquished the
hallmark which best characterizes his theater — his constant reserve of soft emotions and poetical tones —, and this accounts for
the fact that his popularity increased as new concessions to his
audience evolved, though perceptive literary critics continued to
lament the absence of daring inventiveness in his plays. His theater
was no less interesting for its accommodations; it was simply less
original.

I A Satire on Bachelorhood

Only three characters fill the cast listing for *Three in Dim Light*
(*A media luz los tres;* 1953), an amusing theatrical exercise that
Mihura began writing early in 1951. One actress may play all four
female roles, as was the case in the original casting when Conchita
Montés starred as Mariví, Elena, Lulú, and Paca. In turn each
woman visits the bachelor apartment of Alfredo, a vain, self-
appointed authority on women. Alfredo's low opinion of women is
indicated by his frequent references to their mindless habits and
superficial concerns. He leaves his apartment in shambles, for instance, simply to gratify their need to straighten things up. He
keeps cheap liquor to satisfy their undiscriminating taste, and goes

to painful extremes rigging up elaborate devices to trap his naive and unsuspecting female guests into staying with him overnight. This is all theory, however, for his success is minimal. We gain an insight into his deeper insecurities when he explains his sure-fire technique to his married friend, Sebastián, a man curious to learn the secrets of Alfredo's alleged conquests.

The surprise that lies in store for Alfredo, Sebastián, and the audience is that each of the women Alfredo attempts to seduce upends the anticipated triumph and turns the amorous adventure into disaster. The first to arrive is his neighbor, Mariví, who systematically destroys Alfredo's efforts to create a romantic atmosphere by becoming tipsy on his expensive cognac and thus thwarting his sexual advances. Elena is the second "victim." She is married to one of Alfredo's friends and arrives declaring that she is willing to sacrifice everything for an extramarital affair. But Alfredo's bungling leads to his total exasperation; instead of embracing Elena, his comical defeat is exacerbated by the fact that she turns to his friend Sebastián, her former lover, and tries to renew their old affair.

The third "conquest" is that of Lulú, a timid and trusting girl of the streets. Lulú's terrible head cold prevents any physical encounter. Alfredo's offer to rescue her from a sordid life of soliciting strangers in exchange for his affection seems to be an attractive arrangement, but when Lulú's old boyfriend returns unexpectedly, she departs and quickly forgets Alfredo. Each of these amorous mishaps plays havoc with Alfredo's pride. He gradually becomes a beaten, unheroic sad soul, reminiscent of the pathetic little men in Carlos Arniches' grotesque comedies, where human sufferings are overplayed to emphasize the protagonists' comical self-delusions. His pretenses have been uncovered, his hopes shattered, his loneliness made worse. Rejected by three exciting, worldly women, Alfredo finally turns to a simple girl who laughs at his jokes, his own maid, Paca. In the end he marries the much younger and always cheerful Paca, thus settling down to a life of domestic tranquility, another example of a would-be Don Juan trapped by the innocent charms of a naive servant girl.[1]

Three in Dim Light is a comedy of high-level dialogue and low-level situational farce. Intelligently written, it is designed to elicit laughter with clever repartée and surprise happenings. Originally Mihura intended to entitle this piece "Cuarto de soltero" ("Bachelor's Room"), and his sole aim, from the time of its inception through the long run of its commercial success, was to satirize the anti-intellectual trickery that a modern gallant feels compelled to employ in order to trap his female prey. Alfredo does not articulate his libidinous needs well nor clearly, but rather he relies on ingenious devices to accomplish his end, such as an artificial rainmaker that he can switch on outside his balcony whenever his female guest shows signs of wanting to leave.

Mihura also sustains our interest in Alfredo's desperate and pathetic plight by manipulating a certain turn of events in favor of Sebastián, the married friend. Sebastián, without really trying and with little interest in having an extramarital affair, always seems to land new love adventures, while the bachelor Alfredo, despite his meticulous schemes, fails at every turn. Once again Mihura has written a good play based on a simple plot of straight, lineal development. Its success is due in large measure to the sophisticated range of the playwright's dialogue, which one enthusiastic critic has called "exquisite, exemplary, free from coarse jests, comprising a thousand delicious turns, and enriched by the twofold blend of humor and tenderness."[2]

II *A Flimsy Farce About an Eccentric Bullfighter*

La Codorniz contains a number of prototypes of Mihura's future plays. One striking example is the ten-minute playlet entitled *Una corrida intrascendente (An Insignificant Bullfight)*, first published in the pre-Civil War magazine *Gutiérrez*, rewritten for *La Codorniz,* and eventually expanded into the three-act comic farce, *The Case of the Gentleman Dressed in Violet (El caso del señor vestido de violeta; 1954)*.

This play attempts to deal with a bullfighter's severe psychological disturbances. The protagonist, Roberto Zarzalejo, is a highly popular *torero* with intellectual pretensions. His feigned aristocratic mannerisms propel him into a world of snobbery and affectation — giving lectures, attending art exhibits, and participating in social affairs. But his most abnormal problem resides in an intensified "grandmother complex" stemming from a childhood promise to his impoverished grandmother that he would never become a bullfighter. When he did in fact enter the profession, his grandmother disappeared, and Roberto is now a tormented, guilt-ridden schizophrenic who often hallucinates and believes himself to be his own grandmother.

He refuses medical treatment, preferring to conceal his bizarre behavior from all acquaintances, including his fiancée Susana. She, of course, is aware that something is deeply troubling Roberto, and, assuming an attitude of sympathetic dependency, she attempts to demonstrate her love and support. This anxiety only serves to aggravate Roberto's affliction. He hides himself away, fails to appear at the bullring, and glories in the public notoriety his eccentricity has generated. Finally he breaks his engagement to Susana and treats her with contempt.

In desperation, Susana turns to her physician father for help, but he, a great admirer of Roberto's prowess in the bullring, dismisses the matter as unimportant and accords Susana no sympathy. As time passes, Roberto's conduct becomes so strange that a famous psychiatrist is called in for consultation. The noted analyst diagnoses the case as a minimal and curable complex, advising Susana to react to Roberto's histrionics with indifference and the other members of his retinue and household to dissociate themselves from him. This sudden reversal from concern to disinterest in his illness enrages Roberto but provides the needed therapy to strip him of his pomposity and bring him back to normality. Realizing in the end that his fame and false pride are not compatible with a relationship of enduring love, Roberto resumes a life of reality and is reunited with Susana.

As a work of satire, this play has distressed a number of theater critics. One flatly rejects Mihura's unsubtle caricature of the bull-fighter as a stuffy highbrow, stating that the social victim of the satire does not have a generally recognized intellectual bent and that therefore Mihura "satirizes something that does not exist and if he hasn't intended to satirize anything, then we must consider the plan an ingenious game staged in emptiness."[3] Another commentator finds that the resolution of the play's action is faulty, that Mihura erred in his treatment of the bullfighter's psychosis by allowing indifference to cure a serious emotional disturbance.[4] Still other observers uneasily note a regression in this piece to the comically absurd climate of Pedro Muñoz Seca and Enrique Jardiel Poncela, but without the titillating originality of either of those masters.[5] There is, certainly, an unfortunate collapse in the denouement. Roberto's recovery is a medically unsound turn of events, if, in fact, his unstable condition is rooted in a severe emotional ill-

ness. If, on the other hand, Roberto's problem is simply a ploy for
gaining public attention, then the resolution lacks profound meaning. Yet for González Ruiz, these apparent absurdities are unimportant; what holds the play intact, he says, is the internal logic of
its humorous construction and an occasional "flash of gentle
humanity that must move like an underground stream through
authentic humor."[6]

Regardless of its structural inconsistencies, *The Case of the
Gentleman Dressed in Violet* enables Mihura to make fun of bull-
fighting, medicine, psychiatry, love, fear, and social snobbery. It is
a play of obvious satirical aim, limited artistic importance, and
intranscendental social meaning. Overall, it will disappoint upon
serious critical examination of its content, but it will prove gratify-
ing to an audience conditioned to enjoy the laughter that two hours
of light farce can produce.

III   *The Pro-Feminist Statement*

Mihura's ninth play allies his theater with an articulate pro-
feminist attitude found in some earlier comedies of Gregorio Martínez Sierra and Enrique Jardiel Poncela.[7] For the first time in his
own repertory, Miguel Mihura depicts a female protagonist who is
truly liberated.[8]

Set in the year 1895, a time when Spanish women experienced
minimal social freedom, *Sublime Decision* (*Sublime decisión*) deals
with a young woman's pioneer efforts to enter a man's bureaucratic world. Flora Gómez, whom one critic perceptively labels "an
industrial Nora,"[9] is one of two unmarried daughters in a destitute
family. She mocks the pretentious but sacrosanct customs of courtship that accord a woman no human dignity, only to be informed
by her angry aunt that she has sacrificed her one chance for economic security. After learning in secret to operate a typewriter,
Flora announces that she has decided to work full time for a regular
wage. To the complete dismay of her family, friends, and neighbors, she obtains a job at the Energy Ministry. This "sublime decision," prompted by her dire need to escape continued poverty,
brings Flora into open conflict with the norms and mores of social
conformity. Her co-workers at the Ministry view her as a sex
object; her ineffectual father is shamed and revolted by the idea of
his daughter's employment; and her aunt, the domineering and cal-

culating life force of the household, opposes Flora's pragmatic solution to the family's severe financial plight by demanding that she trap a rich husband by whatever lies and deceits she can use.

Flora overcomes the hostility and resistance. She completes her office tasks in record time and astounds the male staff with her thoroughness and competence. Conditions there gradually improve. Courtesy supplants gruffness, flowers and cleanliness replace the clutter, and bureaucratic efficiency improves, thanks to Flora. Everything goes well, that is, until Flora's physical presence and perfume arouse her co-workers to vie for her attention. This problem leads to such internal disorder that the personnel manager discharges her. Immediately her self-righteous family is horrified. Neighbors whisper about a secret sex scandal, friends drop by to increase her sense of shame, and Flora herself becomes embittered and remorseful over the trouble that her desire to work has caused.

Mihura now introduces a *deus ex machina* to extricate his heroine from disgrace. A sudden change in the governmental administration elevates Flora's former boss to the head of the Ministry, and in recognition of Flora's previous work, he creates a new office especially for working women and appoints Flora to direct its operation. Exhilarated anew, she accepts the position. Members of her weak-willed family conveniently put aside their prejudices to take advantage of the glorified status that Flora's efforts have given them. Even her hypocritical aunt acknowledges the wisdom of Flora's "sublime decision," and the play ends with a positive endorsement for the courage that a self-determined woman must exercise to bring about meaningful social change.

The playwright's trenchant satirical forays against male chauvinism, political functionaries, government wages, and middle-class codes of conduct lend this comedy a high degree of social concern less apparent in most of his other plays. The 1895 setting does not restrict his attacks on the more current and seemingly timeless problems of Spain's economic structure, which in this play (as also in *Long Live the Impossible*), Mihura depicts as being incapable of fulfilling the most basic needs of the Spanish working class.[10]

Mihura garnishes *Sublime Decision* with a series of unusual theatrical techniques. His least effective device places the heroine in front of the stage curtain on a number of occasions, whereupon, accompanied by music, she relates parts of the action in lengthy monologues. In his later *Ninette* plays this practice is harmonious with the stage action; in *Sublime Decision* it tends to distract the audience's attention from an engaging plot line. A more ingenious device is the playwright's pairing in Act One of three different groups of women carrying on three simultaneous dialogues. During a pause they change partners and converse again. As author and director, Mihura manipulates the timing of these conversations so they will conclude comically at the same moment. Marion Holt refers to this scene as "a splendid piece of orchestrated nonsense."[11]

Such novel antics of stagecraft had often led Mihura's predecessor, Jardiel Poncela, to essay curious and sometimes bizarre technical experiments in his comedies. It is this similarity to the comic resources of Jardiel's theater that may have induced the eminent critic Alfredo Marquerie to observe that *Sublime Decision* is "of pure Jardielesque stock."[12] Nevertheless, Jardiel used his unique stage effects as an adjunct to the depiction of a grotesque and dehumanized world; Mihura, for his part, while employing a modicum of conversational capers to advance dramatic caricature, seasons that caricature with a much higher level of sympathetic understanding for his characters, a deeper vein of human tenderness, and a more indulgent respect for human follies than we find in the theater of Jardiel.

Despite its incisive social commentary and its acknowledged success as a parody on the kind of value system that once regulated a Spanish woman's total life,[13] *Sublime Decision* remains a static piece of dramatic literature. Vocalized situations prevail over action; one scene generally glides into another without physical movement. The dialogue, for all of its bright and witty properties, tends to repeat itself, and there is a decided unevenness in the play's basic construction. The final scenes, for example, seem to have been dashed off with inordinate haste. They are, declares one observer, "confused, abrupt, and artificial."[14]

Owing to its nineteenth-century backdrop, its gallery of representative personalities from a world of Galdosian figures, and its sharp *costumbrista* focus, the play recalls the poignant writings of Luis Taboada and Sinesio Delgado from the lighthearted pages of *Madrid Cómico*, or the light tones of a Madrilenian *sainete* (one-act farce) that colorful form of dramatic expression which features comical social types and local color.

IV   *The Hollow and Hapless Fiasco*

Canasta (*La Canasta*) remains Mihura's only unpublished play, and rightly so. He calls it "the most sonorous failure" of his repertory. In recent years he has indicated a desire to revise Acts Two and Three, hoping to salvage the essence of the play's sparkling dialogue and to remove multiple defects in its structure, rhythm, and arbitrary characterizations.[15] This flimsy parody on certain permissive activities underlying a modern marriage was so badly received by Mihura's public and so thoroughly berated by his critics that the playwright had it removed from the stage only a few days following its disappointing première in December of 1955. Mihura has since refused to permit circulation or publication of the manuscript.

The play begins well. It deals in Act One with the free-love alliance between Laura, a famous Chilean singer, and Ramón, her blasé gay blade. For fifteen years the couple has carried on an uncomfortable illicit relationship, consisting of frivolous leisure-time activities with other young swingers from a group of *nouveaux riches*. Their daily routine includes outings with snobbish, neurotic, cynical friends, playing canasta, attending cocktail parties, and reveling in boredom. Finally wearied by this metropolitan *dolce vita* existence, Laura and Ramón decide in Act Two to legitimize their relationship and at the same time move into a country chalet. But long years of canasta and cocktail sprees have not equipped either of them for domestic quiescence. Faced with the prospect of inactivity, they turn to other couples for diversions hinging dangerously close to wife- and husband-swapping and sundry games of infidelity. In the final act, convinced that their experiment with countryside matrimony has failed, they determine to move back to their city hotel and resume the fast, swinging pace of their former detachment from conventional responsibilities.

Mihura acknowledges the fact that *Canasta* is an artistically unbalanced work. He also has admitted that the play left too many spectators aghast over the absence of any redeeming social value throughout its development, and that its withdrawal was due mainly to moral considerations. The year 1955 was too early, he states, to satirize the carefree, daring intensity of extramarital games and "kooky" bedroom antics.[16] Few critics openly question the play's moral fiber, however. They seem content to damn it on its tenuous platform of "pasteboard characters," a "heavy, dull rhythm," its "aseptic humor," and "excessive reiterations," as well as its "vague, vulgar, substantially stupid thesis."[17] Marquerie claims that behind all of its extravagance the comedy hides "a tremendous hollowness" of artistic intent.[18] Perhaps Mihura will yet refurbish this hapless tenth play. Until then it will remain a regrettable parenthesis among his other noteworthy productions, a work his admirers should probably choose to ignore.

V A Shallow Satire on Marriage

Madame Renard's Chalet (El chalet de Madame Renard; 1961) is a trivial, sentimental piece that begins with promise and ends in disrepair. It concerns the struggles of an aging and penniless exduchess to remarry for a sixth time and thus dispel the clouds of loneliness that have settled in on her fifty years. The action takes place in Nice, where the protagonist, Madame Renard, a Spanish woman by birth and previously married to five successive Frenchmen, spends her time gambling at the casinos in order to pay off some of her mounting bills. The news of her cousin's recent privation, coupled with the fearful reality of her own straitened circumstances, spurs her to advertise in the local press for a wealthy suitor.

Two middle-aged pretenders answer the ad. Each claims to be a distinguished gentleman of means with bright business prospects on the horizon. In truth they are common charlatans hoping to appropriate the fortune Madame Renard claims to own. The humor of the situation revolves about the lies and deceits the three people resort to with one another. Since Madame Renard cannot make up her mind as to which suitor to marry, she invites both men to remain with her at her chalet for several days. During the course of their stay, the men discover the truth about her embarrassing financial condition, just as Madame Renard had known from the beginning that her guests were penniless crooks but refused to evict them out of a sense of pity. From this time on, the two down-and-out pretenders learn to depend on Madame Renard's flim-flam ingenuity; she is an astute and capable manipulator in her own right, well-endowed after five disastrous marriages with the know-how to resist penury through finagling and finesse. Her supreme act of shrewdness is achieved when she attempts to marry off one of her indigent gentlemen friends to a millionairess. However, the wealthy woman cannot make up her mind which of the two malefactors to marry.

Eventually, Madame Renard contracts another marriage offer, but her suitor turns out to be a distasteful poultry farmer whose crude mannerisms repel her. She is on the brink of accepting his offer, however, just to settle her debts, when an unexpected family fortune descends upon her destitute cousin, saving Madame Renard as well from the humiliation of having to marry beneath her self-assigned level of social grace. The wedding with the poultry farmer is canceled, her male companions are themselves freed from marital consignment, and the trio decides to face the world together, strengthened against loneliness and outside pressures by a mutual trust.

Mihura, himself a solidly confirmed bachelor, singles out the institution of marriage for a constant avalanche of satirical jibes in *Madame Renard's Chalet.* His protagonist's long history of marital miseries had resulted in three divorces and two deaths, while her present efforts to remarry say nothing of love, only convenience. The secondary characters, who generally intrude upon, rather than benefit the main action, also contribute negative examples and statements to deprecate the married state.

The playwright runs into trouble mid-way through his second act. While the satire remains sharp and the dialogue, as always, illuminates and overshadows the action,[19] a heavy dose of sentimentality begins to replace Mihura's subtle irony. Too many emotional concessions encroach upon his gentle intellectual humor, and the ultimate conversion of two crafty rogues into respectable philanthropists is all too predictable. Marquerie deigns to attribute this flaw to "the touching affection of the poet for his creation," a positive feature of the playwright's oft-cited "reserve of emotion and tenderness" superimposed on "a comedy of half-tones and intellectual gaiety." [20]

VI *The Plight of Four Artful Hookers*

One of Mihura's most popular plays, *Maribel and the Strange Family* (*Maribel y la extraña familia*) ran for more than one thousand performances during the 1959–60 theater season. In large measure that comedy's extraordinary success was due to its whimsical depiction of a prostitute and her three co-workers. When, only three years later, Mihura premiered another play dealing with a prostitute and her three companions, the mold was already too familiar, and the comedy, *Ladies of the Night* (*Las entretenidas*, 1962), wilted commercially for having saturated the market with charming streetwalkers. Yet while Mihura's subject matter in *Ladies of the Night* is decidedly similar to the more beguiling *Maribel*, there is a substantial difference of tone in the two plays. *Maribel* is a poetically crisp and genial comedy; *Ladies of the Night* is laden with darker hues of sadness, though creamed with the froth of a less durable plot.

The women in this play seek love rather than sex. Fany and her friends fear that without the solace of continued expense accounts and rent-free living, provided by their more affluent clients, they will be compelled to solicit customers from the street. The specter of unemployment looms large, a constant threat to their security. Accordingly, each of the four girls must learn to manipulate her paramour in order to maintain that small measure of financial support by which she survives. Fany's patron over the past four years has been Don José, a wealthy physician who now wishes to regain his independence. The entire play concerns Don José's earnest attempts to rid himself of Fany and Fany's own clever efforts to keep him. She resorts to various acts of trickery, lies, and cunning, while he counters defensively with lies and deceits of his own. At one moment Fany attempts suicide, but Don José foils her plan by substituting bicarbonate tablets for sleeping pills. On another occasion Don José weaves an elaborate tale about a pregnant girlfriend he must take care of, but Fany discovers the ruse and fights back with a heightened emission of intrigue. When Don José finally gains his freedom, he finds it to be intolerable without Fany. Having trusted a friend to assist him in breaking off with her, he now learns that his self-serving friend has tried to take his place. Desperate to keep her, Don José humbly returns, promising Fany a flow of love and security in return for her affection, and Fany gladly consents. Thus the play ends where it began, with Fany concerned about safeguarding her future relationship with a rich paramour.

Mihura's satire swings cheerfully back and forth among the artful games and countergames of his protagonist's wiles. In this way an ingratiatingly gay current of humor tempers the reserved irony and lightens a faint wisp of bitterness smoldering beneath Fany's desperate struggle to avoid the pain of privation and loneliness. The author's obvious intent to keep his audience laughing all but smothers the sobering vein of Fany's plight and Don José's discomfort, dispelling as well any chance for a balanced sense of serious dramatic tension to emerge. Yet Mihura's technical skill, his pace and precision, his deft architectural maneuvering, are exceptional gifts when we consider that the alternative to this verbal, sophisticated high comedy would be a rueful exercise in melodrama in the hands of a less able playwright.

Mihura weaves the fabric of a prolonged, repetitious situation with consummate expertise, relying exclusively on his powers of dialogue to hold the play together. As weak as the plot and the action appear to those who may scrutinize the flimsy lineal course of each uncomplicated incident, there is an intrinsically sound property in the dialogue to exalt the play and accord it an authenticity worthy of Mihura's best writings. *Ladies of the Night* is a model of Mihura's commercially sensitive genius at work: he has taken a simple situation, tuned it for a farcical recital, and synchronized its every turn to be wholly consonant with his professed aim of extracting two hours of laughter from the audience. While literary distinction often eludes those who traffic with this formula, it has proved beneficial for marketing a commercial product during the Franco era of twentieth-century Spain.

CHAPTER 8

Major Character Studies

IN Mihura's best plays we find a charitable concern for the anti-hero, the vulgar personality. Like Carlos Arniches' memorable characters of the so-called "grotesque tragedy" genre, Mihura's protagonists often agonize under the burden of their own enervated natures or struggle against a code of unrealistic values, not always with success. If they fail to achieve a complete liberation from the inhibiting forces of conformity, they will succumb to the pressures of social living or to the weaknesses inherent in their own tractable natures. Boredom and monotony prevail when they resist working out the freedom within their grasp. The few characters who obtain success in their quest for freedom do so, according to Mihura, at the sacrifice of fond allegiances, careers, or deeply shared human commitments, with a corresponding repudiation of established social values. Love is often a significant factor in their personal struggle for self-mastery; but what counts more is being true to their own ideals. Mihura's message is basically existential in meaning; his protagonists — more often strong women dominating weaker men — must expand their freedom untrammeled by codes or influences beyond the confines of their own dispositions.

I Portrait of a Middle-Aged Pícaro

My Beloved Juan (*Mi adorado Juan;* 1956) is one of Miguel Mihura's most widely read and admired plays. It has been edited and filmed, adapted for television, and translated into a dozen languages. Since earning for Mihura the 1955–56 National Prize for Drama, it has been ranked among the best Spanish comedies of the 1950's and is considered by some critics to be the finest work of both "genuine literary and theatrical interest"[1] to have issued from Mihura's pen.

Part of the play's immense popularity has nothing at all to do with its plot, tone, or action, but grows out of the public's prevailing tendency to equate the character of Juan, the protagonist, with the personality of his creator. Hence, drama critics, biographers, and literary historians frequently turn to *My Beloved Juan* to extract a reasonably accurate portrait of Mihura. While many readers are led to judge Juan as a mere literary representation of the author,[2] they fail to realize that he is also, by Mihura's own admission, the spiritual incorporation of Mihura's fondest dreams and longed-for life-style, his "beloved" alter ego. Juan embodies those attributes of demeanor, dress, and sentiment that have characterized the author's public image and self-concept for many years. He is the prototype of idleness. He dresses as he wishes, combs his hair in any fashion, comes and goes at his own volition, plays dominoes, and never exerts himself. The following passages from Act One promote this self-portrait:

He has no ambitions or needs. His favorite dish is cheese and he sleeps a lot.

He enjoys working for others, but without profiting therefrom and without being noticed. He says that too much work, like overeating, shows a lack of good breeding.

He despises ceremonies and formality.

In all of his movements and even in his manner of speaking one perceives that he belongs to that class of people who are born already a little weary.

First written in 1949 near the end of Mihura's lengthy eighteen-year career as a scriptwriter for the Spanish film industry, *My Beloved Juan* was originally intended for the screen. Following the extraordinary stage success of *Three Top Hats,* Mihura decided to begin revising *My Beloved Juan.* He gradually pruned its many cinematographic settings — a scientific laboratory, a city park, several wharf scenes — and adapted its piquant dialogue to the stage, where it was first performed in January of 1956. The play was received enthusiastically, although several critics were bothered by Mihura's contrived, sentimental ending.[3]

As the play opens, Juan's idyllic and seemingly carefree existence is interrupted by the intrusion of love. He meets Irene, a well-educated and well-to-do young woman whose life until now has been one of assiduous devotion to her father, a reputable biologist named Dr. Palacios, and his arrogant collaborator, Manríquez, both of whom are engaged in an important laboratory experiment. Juan's own educational training is in the field of medicine, but he has forsaken the cloistered activity of scientific research in favor of his own world of poetic fantasy and blithe amusements.

Although Irene cares deeply for her father's labors, her love for Juan compels her to abandon the laboratory for the idler's infectious life-style. This behavior angers Dr. Palacios, who has little tolerance for Juan's debonair attitudes and no patience for his daughter's whim. In addition to her father's reprimands, Irene is faced also with Manríquez's stern disapproval, for he too loves Irene and is disposed to discredit Juan in her eyes. Not wanting to cause a family rift and being sensitive to Irene's heartache, Juan decides to break off their relationship. He absents himself from Irene for nine days, but at the end of this trial separation they both realize that their love is too strong a force to be ignored. When he finally proposes marriage, Juan insists that Irene give up her life of comfort and luxury to embrace his values and pursuits. His conditions are that she must now live in his quarters on the waterfront; that she will tolerate uncomplainingly whatever annoyances or deprivations his life-style may generate; and that she is to grant him complete freedom to live his life as though he were still a bachelor. Irene is obviously not a liberated woman; she readily consents to his terms. She is aware, however, that difficulties will arise and that her love will eventually be put to a supreme test.

In Act Two, Irene's emotional forbearance begins to deteriorate. She and Juan are now married and residing in a cramped, smelly, noisy hovel on the wharf. Juan has succeeded in persuading her to have her fashionable wardrobe altered into clothes more suitable to their spartan way of life. She is denied any chance of attending parties for her now-famous father because Juan detests social gatherings. Although Juan attempts to be gentle and sensitive to her feelings and demonstrates genuine affection for her, he nonetheless holds her firmly to the conditions of their marriage bond.

In the meantime Manríquez has exercised his ambitious cunning to expropriate Dr. Palacios' research findings. With them he intends to go to America to promote his own success and profit. Dr. Palacios, who craves only peace and solace after the hardships of a long arduous career, offers Manríquez no resistance. Hoping to capitalize on Irene's growing discomfort with Juan at their waterfront shack, Manríquez tries to lure her into joining him on the luxury liner that will transport them to a new and exciting life in America. Irene fools everyone, including the audience, into believing she has truly deserted Juan for Manríquez's tempting offer; but in reality she has used the occasion to sneak into Manríquez's stateroom aboard the ship and destroy her father's research documents. Dr. Palacios no longer cares for the papers since he is too old and tired to be ambitious and he has been converted to the carefree, escapist philosophy of his son-in-law's mode of life.

With Manríquez's evil designs thwarted, Irene returns to Juan, willing to adhere to the values of his bohemian world. And Juan, owing to his previous concern over losing Irene to the villain Manríquez, has been aroused sufficiently from his selfish lethargy to concede a willingness to make certain adjustments for her future comfort. He has purchased a new refrigerator, intends to become the neighborhood doctor, and will even consider moving off the wharf when children enter their lives. Thus compromise melds with tender love; the play ends, all too sentimentally, suggesting the triumph of shaky marital bliss over the ignored adversities of a semi-bohemian existence.

Mihura effectively executes a dramatic contrast between Irene and Juan by allowing the tension of their respective strengths and weaknesses to swell into a gradual crescendo. Irene's eventual capitulation may distress contemporary playgoers who experience mortification at the heroine's extreme lack of sexual independence, yet her choice to be a subservient wife— to bend for Juan's sake whenever he so desires, to sacrifice her own career for a life of devotion to her husband — is not only consistent with the character's dependent personality, but it conforms as well to the tide of the social era to which she belongs. One must keep in mind that while Mihura's female protagonists generally are imbued with a high degree of self-determination, they neither struggle for equality with men nor endeavor to secure sexual emancipation from the restrictive customs of a male-oriented social order.

Irene's pledge is to love, to devotion within marriage, and in this respect she transcends a bland conformity to Juan's free-love autocracy. She obliges him to honor the socially acceptable procedure for living together, namely, to marry her. Juan, of course, garners the ultimate victory from this conflict. When Irene repudiates the seductive power of fame and fortune held out to her by Manríquez, and returns to Juan, she does so unconditionally, still euphoric, ever subject to his controlling influence. Her previous tension, frustration, and vacillation prove quite meaningless now, even in view of Juan's moderate, unhurried concessions; indeed, it is interesting to note that when Irene decides to return to her husband, she knows nothing of Juan's intention to acquiesce.

There is an element of Romantic, Byronian license in Juan, a free-wheeling, hippie-style individualism which, added to his endearing personal charm, must account in large measure for the character's popularity. Juan's personality lures the Spanish theatergoer with much the same appeal, though greatly tempered, as the pompous exploits of that timeless legendary reprobate, Don Juan Tenorio, command from a faithful gallery of admirers. Mihura's Juan, for all his smooth grace and sophisticated lovability, and for all the unsung service he renders humanity beneath a camouflage of indifference, is an authentic social cop-out, a veritable anti-hero of middle-aged picaresque dimensions. Like a number of Mihura's male protagonists, his *raison d'être* is nonconformity. Until the final scene of Act Three, he yearns to live on the margin of society, intending to enjoy the comforts of its established order while refusing to play an active role of support for the very system which sustains and nurtures him. Finally he agrees to serve as the neighborhood physician, cracking thereby the mold of his social withdrawal. Though he will probably adhere to his carefree notions and will likewise oblige Irene to render obedience to his code, Juan's love for his wife prompts a partial re-entry into the social order he had previously mocked. Thus the play ends with an affirmative trifold message that rebellion can have a positive value, that compromise is also a virtue, and that love brings a needed dimension of magic and beauty to life.

II *The Genial Prostitute*

Mihura's fertile imagination has produced numerous happy hookers. From the lively, uninhibited Paula of *Three Top Hats* through the friendly and outgoing Fany in *Ladies of the Night* to the effervescent Maribel, the jewel of them all, a grand total of eighteen saucy bargirls, wary streetwalkers, and fun-loving daughters of joy sweeten the pages of no less than six major comedies among Mihura's twenty-two published plays. Only one of his wayward ladies — Nieves, the protagonist of *A No-Account Woman* — is miserable and lonesome. The others are spontaneous extroverts, filled with hope, bubbling over with a gladness for life. They provide a special kind of thematic fascination for their creator. Even their dainty, nymphet names — Nini, Pili, Rufi, Cloti, Juli, Lulú, etc. — bespeak a world aglow with sprightly creatures immersed in cosmetics and lingerie, cheap perfume, and teasing wiles.

Without question the most charming and complicated figure of them all is Maribel, the protagonist whose agonizing metamorphosis from venery into respectability constitutes the theme of *Maribel and the Strange Family* (*Maribel y la extraña familia*). The comedy ran for more than 2,000 performances and was awarded the National Prize for Drama as the best Spanish play of 1959.

Maribel espouses a wanton woman's right to be happy. Her conversion from profligacy to decency is achieved by self-determination, a process requiring an unusually tender and sympathetic dramatic treatment. We first encounter her entering the home of Marcelino, a timid, naive widower whom she had met a few days earlier in a neighborhood bar. It is Marcelino's intention from the beginning to marry Maribel, but he is too simple-minded to realize that her coarse speech, seductive attire, and suggestive manners denote a particular profession that would be convulsively incompatible with his protective upbringing. The uproarious humor of the situation increases when Maribel is introduced to the two women in Marcelino's life, his elderly mother and aunt. They turn out to enjoy rock music and flashy clothes, and thus they are very pleased to meet a modern, vibrant young woman of Maribel's character. Maribel is, of course, extremely nervous and ill at ease. She has come to Marcelino's home with different expectations. She learns that her customer is suddenly a serious suitor, that the two eccentric old ladies are prospective in-laws, and that her accustomed life of soliciting has been replaced by an environment of positive kindness, understanding, and love.

At first Maribel cannot deal with the idea of security and marriage. She displays a myriad of normal reactions, ranging from hostile resistance to an inhibited withdrawal. Unable to cope with the decency and courtesy that surround her, she attributes the family's strange behavior to madness. She then turns to several companions of the profession for advice, but they are predictably suspicious and frightened by the prospect of Marcelino's interest in their friend. They are especially concerned for her well-being when they learn that Marcelino's first wife had drowned under mysterious circumstances. They advise Maribel to drop this absurd notion and flee for her life.

Maribel does not allow her friends' apprehensions to dissuade her from making a break from the sordid existence of her recent past. To allay her own fears about Marcelino's dead wife, she visits his hometown in the provinces. There she learns that the drowning was indeed accidental and that Marcelino is an intrinsically good and honest fellow. Her final crisis is reached when she attempts to reveal her past to Marcelino, but he either chooses to ignore her confession or is too naively oblivious to the truth she is trying to disclose. In the end, Maribel accepts the ideal world he and his family have created for her and joyfully consents to Marcelino's marriage proposal.

The play is a fine example of Mihura's success in depicting inverted values and paradoxical situations where two disparate worlds come together. By society's standards, for instance, Maribel represents at best a victim of circumstances and at worst a morally corrupt individual, yet Miguel Mihura portrays her as a normal and completely moral human being. Her redemption through love is disclosed by gradual changes in her speech and mannerisms. In Act One she uses vulgar expressions common to her tavern and back-alley habitat, but by the third act her language has become precise, refined, correct. The same transformation takes place in her demeanor. She shifts from the typed and caricatured brothel figure of Act One to become a well-rounded personality by the final scenes of Act Three. The "strange family," on the other hand, is a curious admixture of eccentric foolishness and unabashed innocence. While Marcelino represents the straight, decent world of conventional middle-class morality, his sheltered existence reveals a mentality strangely out of step with the changing social scene. The two old ladies, who vividly call to mind the lively spinsters in Joseph Kesselring's *Arsenic and Old Lace,* apply their old-fashioned norms to modern circumstances with the result that they remain ingenuously unaware of reality as it passes by. At the same time, however, they possess none of the destructive prejudices that society would impose upon them to reject Maribel from their midst. The only characters unable to generate any shift in attitude are Maribel's three prostitute friends, Rufi, Pili, and Nini. Though generous and loyal to Maribel, they remain fearful of Marcelino, as they are distrustful of all men, and hence they voluntarily draw back into the shadows of their disreputable world.[4]

The play contains an obvious sentimental appeal as it re-enacts in caricature the redeeming power of love. Mihura wrote it expressly to challenge the theatrical talents of the Venezuelan actress, Maritza Caballero, and he dashed off all three acts in less than two months, "to please the public and, if possible, to please the critics as well."[5] His happy-ever-after conclusion is the natural consequence of a long series of amusing embroilments, modified suspense, and character revelations that respond to the author's explicit intention "to emphasize that innocence, trust, and goodwill can exist where one least expects to find them."[6] *Maribel* is such a lighthearted play that Torrente Ballester exclaimed that even fat ladies enjoyed the illusion of feeling slimmer when they emerged from the theater.[7]

The characters are human and believable. Mihura's indulgent compassion ascribes lovable dimensions to the protagonist, while his gentle and human satire of Marcelino and his doting family stops just short of falling into caricature or farce. For Valencia, the play marks Mihura's maturity as a humorist; it contains "the supreme virtue of a solid literary effort."[8] This virtue is keenly sensed in Maribel's almost mystical struggle for personal redemption. Mihura endows her with a dynamic, intuitive force that gains momentum as Maribel conquers the falseness of her accustomed way of life and decides on her own terms that she will no longer hide the shame of her past indiscretions from Marcelino. In this regard, following Act One, Maribel's words and actions are neither controlled nor exploited for their comical properties. Thereafter Mihura allows his heroine the kind of autonomy that authentic characters must possess if they are to lift themselves above situational dilemmas and whimsical repartee into a sphere of personal magnetism. Owing to her sensibilities and humanity, Maribel is one of Miguel Mihura's few characters to gain a solid footing in that sphere.

III   *An Enduring Literary Achievement*

Lovely Dorotea (*La bella Dorotea;* 1963), is an outstanding serious drama about a young woman's courageous struggle to be loved and respected. When Mihura's somewhat bland and often contrived satirical comedies are no longer staged and when his theater of intrigue has lost its appeal, *Lovely Dorotea* will likely remain as one of his most enduring literary achievements. As Holt contends, "without question this appealing play ranks among the playwright's most original and most consummate works."⁹ It deserves such praise because Dorotea, the protagonist, emerges as a true heroine, a multi-dimensional character whose intrepid search for self-realization transcends the limits of a simple plot to become a universal symbol for any individual's battle — or collectively, a nation's struggle — to resist the leveling forces of a repressive social order.

The play takes place in Zolitzola, a fictitious town in northern Spain, a seaside community steeped in monotony and moral asphyxiation, reminiscent of the world of Benavente's Moraleda, Pérez Galdós' Orbajosa, Clarín's Vetusta, and the provincial locale for Arniches' grotesque tragedy, *Miss Trevélez*. In an atmosphere pregnant with malicious gossip and intellectual torpor, we find Dorotea, a wealthy, proud, and sensitive woman, about to be married. Suddenly she confronts the worst crisis of any bride's life, a dilemma of sufficient magnitude to devastate for all time her sense of pride and personal worth. On the very day of her wedding, she is jilted. Her reaction to this public humiliation forms the core of the play's subsequent development. Dorotea refuses to retreat into the protective sanctuary of her home. Instead she determines to parade her monumental hurt in a nonchalant manner before the town's wondering gaze. Still dressed in her wedding gown, a symbol of her tenacious quest for another man, she strolls up and down the streets of Zolitzola for nearly seven months. At first the townspeople avoid her, then their awe turns to ridicule, and finally they conspire to have her committed to an asylum.

The hostile forces in Dorotea's midst are represented first by her Aunt Rita, a treacherous widow who hopes to expropriate the family property when Dorotea is declared insane; then by Dorotea's so-called friends — Benita, Inés, and Remedios —, three hypocritical gossipmongers whose shallow minds and spiteful tongues make them suitable candidates to be Dorotea's most de-vious enemies. Their continual efforts to sabotage her personal crusade bring derision upon the household and begin to erode Dorotea's self-esteem.

Only Rosa, Dorotea's trusted maid and confidante, while she does not fully understand her mistress, stands by her throughout the long months of the aunt's finagling and the three girls' un-ceasing mockery. Dorotea has just about reached the breaking point when she meets a handsome stranger whose own past is an embarrassment to him and who initially conspires to obtain Dorotea's family fortune by marrying her. Although she is pain-fully aware that José, the new man in her life, harbors this nefarious plan, she nonetheless consents to be his wife. She is by now so desperate to extricate herself from her plight that even a fleeting illusion of happiness with an untrustworthy man looms as an acceptable alternative.

By Act Three, Dorotea and José are married, and she has gained thereby a fragile respite from the injurious criticism of Aunt Rita and the three conspirators. The society which once scorned her is now obliged to accept and to forgive her flagrant display of arro-gance on the public streets. But her own distrust of José, who by virtue of their union now has control of her entire estate, under-mines Dorotea's sense of well-being. Several false clues increase her suspicions of her husband, but to her great joy she ultimately learns that he is now genuinely in love with her and has no intention of leaving. The play ends on the positive note that Dorotea's marriage as well as her re-integration into the social milieu are secure and lasting attainments.

Dorotea evolves out of a fusion of deceptive responses to the reality of her being. Unlike our early and accurate apprehension of the aunt and the three friends as irreparably perfidious creatures, we do know Dorotea instantly. Her personality unfolds by degrees, in consonance with the progressive ebb and flow of the play's action. First she appears as an arrogant, rebellious nonconformist, deliberately at odds with the ossified mentality of her town, content to enjoy the freedom that a self-proclaimed independence of thought and action confer upon her. At her wedding celebration she feigns indifference, even a smug intolerance, for the events in progress — a protective pose that shields the nervous tension welling up within her.

When jilted, the authentic Dorotea, deeply wounded, hides beneath the air of nonchalance. Vowing to shed her wedding dress — her "uniform," as she calls it — only when she encounters a new suitor, she continues to bury her inner anguish under an unyielding façade of composure. Ultimately, when her symbolic gesture becomes a public nuisance and the town plots to put her away, her torment begins to filter out, and the haughty, flippant exterior verges upon collapse. Following her marriage, she must again disguise her true feelings, feigning contentment to conceal inner fears of abandonment. In a touching finale which Mihura carefully controls to avoid concluding his play in a splash of sentimentality, Dorotea breaks down; her tears betray for the first time her joy in knowing true happiness. The emotional masks, like the wedding dress before them, are left behind. The pain subsides, and the heroine is at peace with the world.

Dorotea's nature is thus revealed as a dual profile: the Dorotea of appearances and the Dorotea of inner turmoil. This interplay of pretense masking reality often deludes the spectator, who finds the plot seeming to turn in one direction when the facts of Dorotea's distress intrude to take it in another. The other characters remain basically static, their words and conduct circumscribed by unchanging hypocrisy. The fact that Mihura restricts his antagonists to function within a rigidly mechanized configuration adds greater symmetry and depth to the dynamics of Dorotea's role. There is a danger, of course, in sacrificing the personality of all but his main character for the idea, a risk the playwright also ran with his delineation of a strong Flora towering over her stratified antagonists in *Sublime Decision*. The difference here is that Dorotea is simply a more complete character; her silent suffering and magnanimous nature draw our attention away from the more narrow and unchanging aspect of her enemies: their envy, their meddling, their mischief.

The playwright made great efforts to give a special flavor of artistic distinction to this important play. He introduces various theatrical devices to intensify its mood and to mirror the heroine's inner struggles. One such device is the constant sound of falling rain. A summer storm, complete with thunder and howling winds rages outside Dorotea's home throughout most of the production, a complement to the gloom which has descended on Dorotea's spirit. The unabating rain likewise represents the unrestrained fury of the town's hypocrites as they lash out at Dorotea and attempt to bring her down to their level. Allusions to the sea and a faraway boat also enhance the symbolic value of *Lovely Dorotea*. The protagonist, in her yearning to escape the pain and discomfort of her lonely crusade, longs for the life of serenity suggested by the calm ocean waters. The offstage sounds of dance music contribute as well to her restless desire for a temporary release from suffering.

Marquerie considers the play to be a composite of unquestionable literary virtues. He was the first drama critic to perceive a definite application of quixotic symbolism in Dorotea's transformation from a disillusioned, jilted bride into a self-reliant idealist: "Just as the Knight of the Sad Countenance sallied forth through the fields of La Mancha ... disguised as a knight errant, ... the protagonist of this delightful theatrical work strolls through the streets of her native town dressed in a hardly customary manner ... and is taken for a lunatic and for a rebel."[10] Marquerie also finds in the loyal maid, Rosa, a female variant to Sancho Panza as collaborator and confidante. We should add to this enumeration of literary traits the resemblance of Dorotea's three malicious friends to a functional traditional chorus; they appear at the beginning of each act, representing the voice of social censure against the protagonist. They thereby serve the double function of providing Mihura with a concentrated target for his satire on hypocrisy and provincial mentality and of endowing the comedy with the classical structure of a choric body commenting upon the action.

IV *The Playwright's Choice*

Mihura's two Ninette comedies exemplify the familiar game played between the public's demands for shallow entertainment and the artist's willingness to concede to those demands. When the play *Lovely Dorotea* neared its completion, Mihura was commissioned to write a new commercial hit for the following fall season. As we have observed, *Lovely Dorotea* is a play of superior literary merit, but as a stage production it represented a disappointing business venture. Mihura's audiences were simply not all that enthusiastic over a serious drama about self-sacrifice, meagerly endowed with the kind of high-class humor for which Mihura is internationally noted. Therefore, as he undertook the composition of his commissioned play, *Ninette and a Gentleman From Murcia*

(*Ninette y un señor de Murcia*), the playwright was keenly sensitive to the market value of laughter. He consequently molded five characters into a single amusing situation, assigned them lines of extraordinary fluidity and crispness, and allowed that inimitable current of expanding Mihurian wit and human tenderness to flow over them. The result was a predictable triumph for the Spanish bourgeois theater of frivolity, farce, and badinage.

Ninette and a Gentleman From Murcia ran for one entire year, including the summer season. Its more than 2,000 performances set a record as Mihura's most successful commercial play. It came as no surprise, therefore, that *Ninette* was subsequently awarded the Calderón de la Barca Prize as the best Spanish play of 1964 — Mihura's fourth National Drama award. The playwright thereafter declared *Ninette* to be his favorite play among all his writings for the legitimate stage: "You know," he said in a personal interview in January of 1975, "I prefer *Ninette* because it made me a wealthy man. I am indebted to *Three Top Hats* because Dionisio and Paula brought me a firm and lasting recognition, but I eat and drink and live well today because of my *Ninette*. After *Three Top Hats* I remained hungry and penniless." Mihura's comment singles out one of the serious problems that underlies the oft-repeated "crisis" of the post-Civil War Spanish theater.

The first Ninette play concerns a gullible Spaniard's involvement with a vivacious French girl in Paris. Its sequel, *Ninette, Paris Fashions* (*Ninette, modas de París*), treats the events that transpire between the two after they are married and have relocated in Murcia. The gentleman in question is named Andrés, a rather docile and insecure young man who temporarily leaves the operation of a small religious bookstore in Murcia to visit the French capital on a two-week quest for amorous excitement. With the help of his hometown friend, Armando, he secures lodging in a boarding house run by a Spanish couple in exile. Pedro, the landlord, is a delightful old cynic with antiquated revolutionary ideas. His wife is Bernarda, a less colorful adornment who tolerates Pedro's political harangues and caters to his blustering demands. Their twenty-three-year-old daughter is Ninette, a very determined and beguiling young woman whose vivacity is sharply contrasted with Andrés' timid nature. This contrast between the female protagonist and her male counterpart is one of Mihura's favorite designs for character delineation. We first observed it in the juxtaposition of an audacious, free-spirited Paula and the naive and retiring Dionisio in *Three Top Hats,* and it has re-appeared as a constant thematic device throughout Mihura's productions.

The crux of the humorous situation in *Ninette* lies in Andrés' futile efforts to see Paris and the girl's persuasive control in keeping him home with her. Ninette completely dominates Andrés, using sweet lies, tender wiles, and direct passion to snare her prey. Armando, the Murcian friend, tries desperately to liberate Andrés, but to no avail. Over a month passes, and Andrés is still a prisoner in the boarding house. He eats only Spanish meals, must endure Pedro's political carping, and meekly succumbs to Ninette's seductive charms.

When it finally appears that Andrés will have his first night out on the town, Ninette delivers her coup de grâce: she announces her pregnancy. The girl's father, while of a liberal bent in his politics, is a die-hard traditionalist as to morality, and he insists that Andrés marry Ninette at once. He thereby determines that Andrés and Ninette will live in Murcia and that he and Bernarda will move in with them. Andrés, of course, who has come to Paris for a breezy fling, is in a state of utter panic. He concocts with Armando a plan to escape the clutches of his new-found family, but Ninette again intervenes and lures him back. Andrés spends his last night in Paris at the boarding house with Ninette, and thus the play concludes, reaffirming the multiple limitations and singular achievement of Andrés' Parisian adventure.

The popular success of *Ninette and a Gentleman from Murcia* prompted Mihura to follow soon after with a sequel. Andrés' total subjugation is defined in a second comedy, *Ninette, Paris Fashions.* Ninette now manipulates him to satisfy her personal interests, the chief of which is to open a dress shop in Murcia and sell fashionable French clothes. Andrés is furious with her, not only because a working wife is a public embarrassment to his male pride, but also because the new business means that his own life must be drastically rearranged. Owing to the friction between them, Ninette denies Andrés his conjugal rights, and he in turn begins an open love affair with Maruja, the shop girl in his religious bookstore.

Ninette eventually emasculates Andrés on every front. She takes away his mistress by insisting that the time is ripe for conception — her first pregnancy, the one that trapped Andrés into marriage, had miscarried. She then decides to convert the religious store into an automobile dealership where Andrés will be under the employ of her father, Pedro. Thus Andrés is denied business autonomy. The upshot of Ninette's strong, energetic dominance is the complete enslavement of the hapless Andrés, and this process alone accounts for the play's comic impact. *Ninette, Paris Fashions* is a rather tedious variation on the original theme: Ninette's aggressive superiority and the abdication of Andrés' freedom and destiny. The author's view of matrimony in both plays is overwhelmingly negative. Ninette's pre- and post-marital wars with Andrés are motivated by her dauntless personal need to gain control over her lover and husband.

Yet Ninette is not featured as a relentless shrew or odious tyrant. Her admirable qualities and interests command respect throughout both plays, especially as her intuitive understanding of Andrés' pathetic shortcomings evinces the awakening of a truly emancipated woman. Regrettably, though, her characterization is shallow and one-dimensional. She lacks the depth of a Maribel or a Dorotea because the psychological essence of her frank and forward behavior is too often sacrificed to the advantage of a whimsical situation. Mihura prefers to gain greater mileage with the comical depiction of the anarchistic Pedro, through whom a series of subtle social and political observations escape,[11] than to penetrate beneath the surface of his protagonist's passionate conduct. As such his heroine, for all her charm, remains a flat character in a set of entertaining light comedies. The second play is nothing more than a mechanical parody on the first, and neither adds solid stature to the enduring value of the playwright's literary reputation.

CHAPTER 9

Conclusion

M IGUEL Mihura's creative energies span forty years of theater
activity. From box-office assistant to magazine director, from
illustrator to screenwriter, from collaborator to independent playwright, his work has touched many aspects of the contemporary
theater scene. Directly or indirectly, there are few Spanish plays of
our time that do not owe something to his repertory and craft.

We have seen the extent to which his labor affects the development of two diverse attitudes in the expression of dramatic humor.
His first writings for the stage represent a highly unconventional
form of theatrical art, best characterized by *Three Top Hats* and his
first two plays of collaboration; the majority of his subsequent
comedies reflect an aesthetic compromise to please the large majority with a more traditional format of dramatic structure and
humoristic inventiveness.

Approximately one-third of Mihura's productions are memorable literary accomplishments. They testify to the effectiveness of
applying sophisticated humor to dramatic art, of infusing superb
dialogue with the magic of poetic tenderness and a profound sense
of humanity. They deal primarily with a smiling acceptance of
reality, an admission that human predicaments are not always sur-
mountable, that ideals and illusions are worthwhile commodities of
the spirit, though rarely leading to a satisfying fulfillment. Even his
less successful plays affirm that a life of regulated conformity or
spiritless resignation to routine is wholly intolerable, that there are
merits to be gained through personal emancipation from the con-
stricting forces of habit, social conformity, and selfish pursuits.
Mihura frequently clarifies this moral stance by contrasting the
narrow-minded reality of an orthodox middle-class society to the
free-thinking and free-wheeling expressions of a capricious, informal, and extraordinary world. The conflicts resulting from this

127

confrontation of two opposing milieux and their corresponding characters represent the essence of Mihura's provocative humor.

He began his career promoting incongruous verbal nonsense to elucidate a serious problem in human communication, namely, the gradual disintegration of language into empty formulas and senseless clichés. Once this intellectually-oriented phase of his early writings had run its course, economic necessity prompted his adopting a less bizarre literary pose. We have taken the position in this study that without the audacity and the universal repute of those early contributions, it is doubtful that Mihura would rank today as Spain's leading dramatic humorist. Indeed, that initial period becomes increasingly more significant in the total evaluation of his literary career; as drama critics, literary historians, theatergoers, readers, and professors of drama assess the course of the contemporary Spanish theater's development, their acclamation for the artistry, originality, and spontaneity of Mihura's early productions far outrival their praise for the merits of his later writings of compromise and concession.

During the same year that Mihura premiered his twenty-third and final play for the legitimate stage, one of Spain's most esteemed and influential writers declared that his best plays will endure because they possess universal values and an intellectual humor. On that basis alone Miguel Mihura must be considered "the greatest exponent of current humorous drama."[1]

Notes and References

Chapter One

1. Miguel Mihura, *Obras completas* (Barcelona, 1962), p. 20.
2. *Ibid.*
3. *Ibid.*, p. 27.
4. Joaquín Aguirre Bellver, "Miguel Mihura, o el grillo en el hogar," *Madrid* (November 25, 1961), p. 9.
5. See Mihura, *Obras,* p. 30.
6. See *Primer Acto,* No. 9 (Madrid, July-August, 1959), pp. 4–5.
7. According to Mihura, the attempt by some critics to ascribe the inspiration for his play to Chesterton's Father Brown is wholly erroneous.
8. Personal interview with Mihura, June 9, 1967.
9. *Primer Acto,* No. 9 (Madrid, July-August, 1959), p. 5.
10. See José Monleón, "Ficha de Miguel Mihura," *Miguel Mihura,* ed. Monleón (Madrid, 1965), pp. 31–33.
11. Six of Mihura's other plays have also been filmed, namely, *Long Live the Impossible, Neither Poor nor Rich..., Sublime Decision* (under the title *For Men Only*), *Carlota, Peaches and Syrup,* and *Maribel and the Strange Family.* Unlike *My Beloved Juan* and *A No-Account Woman,* they were adapted for the cinema after earlier stage productions. Television filming has also brought twelve of his plays to TVE (Spanish television) since 1966.
12. See A. D. Olano, *El Alcázar* (Madrid, April 4, 1953), p. 5.
13. See Fernando Lara and Diego Galán, "Miguel Mihura, burgués con espíritu de 'clochard'," *Triunfo,* No. 500 (April 29, 1972), p. 43.
14. See Ricardo Domenech, "Reflexiones sobre la situación del teatro," *Primer Acto,* No. 42 (1963), p. 7.
15. Domingo Pérez Minik, "Itinerario patético de una generación de dramaturgos españoles," *Insula,* Nos. 224–25 (July-August, 1965), p. 3.
16. Evaristo Acevedo, *Teoría e interpretación del humor español* (Madrid, 1966), pp. 107–10.
17. Manuel Diez Crespo, *Primer Acto,* Nos. 29–30 (Madrid, December 1961–January 1962), p. 9.
18. Miguel Mihura, "El teatro de Mihura visto por Mihura," *Primer Acto,* No. 3 (Madrid, 1957), p. 12.
19. Mihura's concept of dramatic humor indicates his aversion to conforming to a stereotyped format. Humor, he says, is not a literary for-

mula, but rather a way of being, a way of expressing oneself, a way of responding to life. See *Primer Acto,* No. 9 (July-August, 1959), pp. 4–5.

20. Ángel Laborda, *Informaciones* (Madrid, September 29, 1959), p. 8.

21. Information conveyed in personal interview, June 9, 1967.

22. 'Córdoba', "Córdoba interroga a Miguel Mihura," *Pueblo* (Madrid, April 4, 1953), p. 15.

23. In Brussels, the traditional rehearsal time of ten in the morning had to be changed to late afternoon in deference to Mihura's mid-morning and noonday siestas. See J. Aguirre Bellver, *Madrid* (November 25, 1961), p. 9.

24. Rafael Cotta Pinto, *La Estafeta Literaria,* No. 178 (October 1, 1959), p. 24.

Chapter Two

1. See, for instance, the importance accorded them in J. Rof Carballo *et al., El teatro de humor en España* (Madrid, 1966), pp. 35–44, 49, 61, 67–81, 87–104, 109–19, 221, 242, 256–58, and 267–68.

2. This concept is defined in Chapter 6 of D. R. McKay, *Carlos Arniches* (New York: Twayne, 1972), pp. 86–101.

3. Miguel Mihura, *Obras completas* (Barcelona, 1962), p. 25.

4. Pedro Salinas, *Literatura española siglo XX* (Mexico: Editorial Séneca, 1941), p. 196.

5. Nicolás González Ruiz, "El teatro de humor del siglo XX hasta Jardiel Poncela," in Carballo *et al., op. cit.,* p. 38.

6. Enrique Díez-Canedo, "Panorama del teatro español desde 1914 hasta 1936," *Hora de España,* XVI (Madrid, April, 1938), p. 28.

7. Alfredo Marquerie, *Veinte años de teatro en España* (Madrid, 1959), p. 56.

8. Rafael Vásquez Zamora, "Tipos y escenas de Arniches," *Insula,* No. 81 (1952), p. 12.

9. García Álvarez shared over 100 titles with some twelve other playwrights. His professional collaborations with both Arniches and Muñoz Seca suggests that their mutual affinities of ideas and aesthetic precepts are perhaps more deliberate than coincidental.

10. The name *astracán* (astrakhan) was appropriated from a short farcical piece co-authored by García Álvarez in which a ridiculous fur hat and coat of astrakhan material were worn. The name is still applied to single out contrived sketches, void of serious intention, which depend entirely on puns, jests, plays on words, absurd repartee, and dislocated speech for their effect, rather than on character delineation or clever plot line. In the hands of García Álvarez the *astracán* is totally innocuous, bearing no hint of political or social parody. It is likewise far removed from recognizable topics of the day, excepting an obvious exploitation of

the comic possibilities in colloquial expressions. It endeavors to render atypical the normal pose and the conventional speech of ordinary conversation by means of a travesty on clichés and platitudes.

11. Mihura, *Obras*, p. 25.

12. González Ruiz, *op. cit.*, p. 39.

13. Information conveyed in a personal interview with Miguel Mihura, June 9, 1967.

14. See Pedro Muñoz Seca, *Obras completas*, ed. José María Bernáldez (Madrid: Ediciones FAX, 1954), Vol. I.

15. González Ruiz, *op. cit.*, p. 39. He designates the years 1912 to 1936 as the literary "lifetime" of the *astracán*. The year 1912 represents the première of *Trampa y carbón*, Muñoz Seca's first conscious effort as an independent playwright to foster the genre. He thereafter assiduously cultivated the *astracán* until his assassination in 1936.

16. Ángel Valbuena Prat, *Historia del teatro español* (Barcelona: Noguer, 1956), p. 63.

17. Alfonso Paso, "Muñoz Seca: El astracán, género de abrigo," *La Estafeta Literaria,* Nos. 282–83 (Janurary 4–18, 1964), p. 54.

18. Mihura, *Obras*, p. 25.

19. See Pedro Muñoz Seca, *op. cit.*, Vols. II–VII. Nearly half of those fifty-five productions were written in collaboration with Pedro Pérez Fernández.

20. Quoted in Alfonso Paso, *op. cit.*, p. 54.

21. Enrique Jardiel Poncela, "Lectura de cuartillas," *Tres comedias con un solo ensayo* (Madrid: Biblioteca Nueva, 1934), p. 25.

22. Paso, *op. cit.*, pp. 54–56.

23. Mihura, *Obras*, p. 25.

24. José Montero Alonso, *Pedro Muñoz Seca: Vida, ingenio y asesinato de un comediógrafo español* (Madrid: Ediciones Españolas, 1939).

25. Gonzalo Torrente Ballester, *Teatro español contemporáneo* (Madrid: Guadarrama, 1957), p. 36.

26. Gonzalo Torrente Ballester, "Cincuenta años de teatro español y algunas cosas más," *Escorial: Revista de cultura y letras,* No. 10 (August, 1941), pp. 275–77.

27. Juan Chabás, *Literatura española contemporánea* (La Habana: Editorial Cultural, 1952), p. 641.

28. Among the writers who represent this view are Enrique de Mesa, Melchor Fernández Almagro, Alfredo Marqueríe, Cristóbal de Castro, Ángel Valbuena Prat, and Emiliano Diez-Echarri.

29. Nicolás González Ruiz, *La cultura española en los últimos veinte años: El teatro* (Madrid: Instituto de Cultura Hispánica, 1949), p. 27.

30. Francisco García Pavón, "Inventiva en el teatro de Jardiel Poncela," in J. Rof Carballo *et al., op. cit.,* p. 89.

31. Domingo Pérez Minik, *Teatro europeo contemporáneo; su libertad y compromisos* (Madrid: Guadarrama, 1961), p. 298.

32. For an analysis of Jardiel's theater, with a summary of the critical studies of most value on Jardiel, see D. R. McKay, *Enrique Jardiel Poncela* (New York: Twayne, 1974).

33. Alfredo Marquerie, *El teatro de Jardiel Poncela* (Bilbao: Ediciones de Conferencias y Ensayos, 1945), p. 27.

34. Marquerie stood virtually alone in his praise for Jardiel. His first brief study (1945) was published at a time of extreme critical furor against the playwright. Marquerie's constant devotion to the writer did most to sway public and critical opinion in his favor. The term *Jardielismo* is used today to designate the entire absurdist trend from Arniches through Jardiel to Miguel Mihura.

35. Alfredo Marquerie, "Jardiel y el Jardielismo," *La Estafeta Literaria,* No. 312 (February 27, 1965), p. 19.

36. Remarks related in a personal interview with Mihura, June 9, 1967.

37. *Ibid.*

38. Juan R. Castellano, "El teatro español desde 1939," *Hispania,* XXXIV (August, 1951), p. 242.

39. In an interview with Manuel Diez Crespo, recorded in *Primer Acto,* Nos. 29–30 (December 1961–Jaunary 1962), p. 9, Mihura stated: "Although one does not always realize who are the writers who make an impression, something always remains from one's reading. Nevertheless, I do not believe that any of them, specifically, has influenced me."

40. Information obtained from Mihura's personal correspondence, through an interview of June 9, 1967.

Chapter Three

1. Evaristo Acevedo, *Teoría e interpretación del humor español* (Madrid, 1966), p. 250.

2. *La Ametralladora* means "The Machine Gun." The magazine was originally called *La Trinchera* ("The Trench"), but that title was dropped after the second issue when it was discovered that the enemy had adopted an identical name for a similar journal.

3. From January 18 through July 4, 1937, the magazine sold for fifteen centavos per copy. Thereafter, until the final issue dated June 26, 1938, the price was increased to 25 centavos. Throughout its short history, however, *La Ametralladora* was distributed free to members of the infantry.

4. *La Ametralladora,* No. 4 (February 8, 1937), p. 1. A later issue defined its purpose "to relieve our soldiers from their long hours of war, to distract them and make them smile, for there is nothing that tones up the spirit, after faith in the cause and in victory, as recreational reading." See No. 23 (July 4, 1937), p. 3.

5. The issue for October 24, 1937 contains an impassioned article of encouragement to the editors written by the young drama critic Alfredo Marquerie. See *La Ametralladora,* No. 39, p. 13. Eight months later, page one of the final issue carries a bold print announcement stating: "Franco is the Caudillo of the war. Franco will know how to guide us in every moment along the difficult roads to peace." See *La Ametralladora,* No. 74 (June 26, 1938), p. 1.

6. *Gutiérrez* was a weekly magazine also, founded in 1927 by the humorist "K-Hito." Its chief contributors were Mihura, Jardiel Poncela, Tono, López Rubio, González Dalmáu, Edgar Neville, and Fernando Perdiguero. The journal folded at the outbreak of the Spanish Civil War.

7. There is no consistent effort on Mihura's part to list credits, either for himself or for members of his staff. The one-page dramatic sketches, when signed at all, carry nonsense names such as "El cabo de cuarto" and "El 710." Some of the signed playlets in *La Ametralladora,* frequently with pseudonyms, are attributed to José María de Vega, Luis de Garay, and José Simón Valdivielso.

8. *La Codorniz* first appeared on June 8, 1941 and consisted then of only fourteen pages. The cost per issue was fifty centavos. With issue number 51, dated May 24, 1942, the price doubled to one peseta and its size, by the end of that year, had increased by ten pages.

9. Juan Guerrero Zamora, *Historia del teatro contemporáneo,* III (Barcelona, 1962), p. 178.

10. Jardiel's first signed contribution to *La Codorniz* is a prose parody on a Sherlock Holmes mystery, "The Thirty-Eight and a Half Murders of Hull Castle." See *La Codorniz,* No. 51 (May 24, 1942), pp. 9–11; 14–18.

11. Don Ramón's first series of *greguerías* for *La Codorniz* appear under the titles "Ramonismo," in No. 133 (December 19, 1943), p. 19; "Mentiras," in No. 135 (January 2, 1944), p. 3; "Greguerías nuevas," in No. 137 (January 16, 1944), p. 3; and "Ramonismo," in No. 139, (January 30, 1944), p. 16; with many thereafter.

12. Some of the notable arguments and responses from both camps are reproduced in Evaristo Acevedo, *Treinta años de risa (1940–1970),* (Madrid, 1973), pp. 169–77. Salient aspects of the polemic are also mentioned throughout Diego Galán, *¿Reírse en España? (El humor español en el banquillo),* (Valencia, 1974).

13. Diego Galán, *op. cit.,* pp. 35–36.

14. Pedro Laín Entralgo, "El humor de *La Codorniz,*" in *La aventura de leer* (Madrid, 1946), p. 129. Pérez Minik has suggested that at some later date the humor of *La Codorniz* may be evaluated as a serious document, capable of interpreting an era of twentieth-century Spanish life. See Domingo Pérez Minik, *Debates sobre el teatro español contemporáneo* (Santa Cruz de Tenerife, Canarias, 1953), p. 282.

15. Cited in Acevedo, *Teoría e interpretación . . . ,* p. 251.

16. José Monleón writes that he has encountered "many positive and even revolutionary elements" in *La Codorniz* of Mihura's epoch, but by "revolutionary" he refers only to a systematic skepticism and the tone of prevailing doubt about the values people generally esteem, a posture analogous to Jardiel Poncela's sardonic jibes at the human race. *La Codorniz* provides no hint of political criticism. See Monleón, "La crítica ante la obra de Miguel Mihura," *Miguel Mihura,* ed. José Monleón (Madrid, 1965), p. 53.

17. *La Codorniz,* No. 45 (April, 1942), p. 1.

18. Miguel Mihura, *Obras completas* (Barcelona, 1962), p. 36.

19. Ángel Zúñiga, *Una historia del cine,* II (Barcelona: Ediciones Destino, 1948), p. 365.

20. Ignacio Soldevila Durante, "Sobre el teatro español de los últimos veinticinco años," *Cuadernos Americanos,* CXXVI, No. 1 (January-February, 1963), p. 276.

21. Miguel Mihura, "De viaje," *La Codorniz* (March 15, 1942).

22. Translated from Eugène Ionesco, *Théâtre* (Paris: Editions Gallimard, 1954), p. 30.

23. Mihura denies that the two writings have a common source. He does admit, however, that during certain periods of his administration of *La Ametralladora* and *La Codorniz* he utilized materials from Italian writers, but never as a part of his signed articles or playlets. His *teatrillos,* he claims, are entirely original (interview with the playwright, June, 1967). Ionesco, for his part, denies that the fourth scene of *La Cantatrice Chauve* had a previous literary source. He states that the recognition scene is based on an actual surprise encounter with his wife on the Metro in Paris. See *The Observer* (London, July 14, 1958). We conclude therefore that whatever resemblance exists between the two writings is an unintended coincidence.

24. *La Codorniz* nearly folded in 1952 due to excessive polemics, internal strife on the staff, and fines. Under Laiglesia's direction (since 1944), the magazine gradually adopted a posture of contemporary social criticism. It focused its humorous barbs on a world in disintegration, a fact which irritated Mihura to the point of his writing two *cartas polémicas* ("polemical letters") to Laiglesia to express his discomfiture and to renounce his collaboration once and for all. Laiglesia's realist tendency, explicitly sustained to the present day, is a definite departure from the so-called *humor codornicesco* of Mihura's tenure, whose humor Laiglesia labels "escapist" in nature.

25. Mihura, "Primera carta a Álvaro de Laiglesia," reproduced in *Miguel Mihura,* ed. José Monleón (Madrid, 1965), pp. 117–19.

Chapter Four

1. Miguel Mihura, *Obras completas* (Barcelona, 1962), p. 25.

2. Two informative studies of Calvo-Sotelo's theater remain unpublished as doctoral theses. See Arturo Jiménez-Vera, "Humor y moralidad en el teatro de Joaquín Calvo-Sotelo" (University of Arizona, 1972); and Ernest C. Rehder, "Thesis Plays of Joaquín Calvo-Sotelo" (University of Florida, 1971).

3. This is the only instance of censorship for political reasons in Mihura's published repertory. The playwright also experienced slight difficulties with Spanish censorship on moral grounds, as for example the stipulation in 1953 that he append an epilogue to the morally suspect third-act ending of *Three in Dim Light*. His unpublished comedy, *Canasta,* was also strongly frowned upon.

4. Mihura insists that the mechanics of laughter reside in the element of surprise. See his interview with Gladys Crescioni Neggers, "Miguel Mihura: Iniciador del teatro del absurdo," *La Estafeta literaria,* No. 572 (September 15, 1975), pp. 9–11.

5. J. Lozano, "¡El circo! Historia, andanzas y aventuras," *Teatro,* XIX (May-August, 1956), 29–33, 73. See also Alfredo Marquerie, "El circo y su festival mundial en España," *Teatro,* XXI (January-March, 1957), 26–27.

6. Mihura, *Obras,* pp. 30–31.

7. Calvo-Sotelo and Mihura, *¡Viva lo imposible! o El contable de estrellas* (Madrid: Edición de los autores, 1951), pp. 93, 95.

8. Another circular treatment in modern Spanish drama, broadened to encompass thirty years and several family units, is forcibly drawn by Antonio Buero Vallejo in his well-known play, *Story of a Stairway* (1949).

9. Mihura, *Obras,* pp. 35–36.

10. Manuel Diez Crespo, "Crítica," *Arriba* (Madrid, December 18, 1943), p. 4.

11. M. Sánchez Camargo, *El Alcázar* (Madrid, December 18, 1943), p. 2.

12. Gonzalo Torrente Ballester, "El teatro serio de un homorista," in J. Rof Carballo *et al., El teatro de humor en España* (Madrid, 1966), p. 20.

13. Evaristo Acevedo, *Teoría e interpretación del humor español* (Madrid, 1966), p. 250.

14. Mihura, *Obras,* p. 37.

15. Marquerie states that *Neither Poor nor Rich* "is like a pause of disjointed and absurd charm in the middle of a panorama covered with the ashes of vulgarity." See *En la jaula de los leones: Memorias y crítica teatral* (Madrid: Ediciones Españolas, 1944), p. 156. Pérez Minik claims that the play is "the best work of humor on the post-war Spanish stage. . . . Its living texture and style is removed from any foreign influence, from any traditional inheritance. . . ." See *Teatro europeo contemporáneo* (Madrid: Guadarrama, 1961), p. 423. Clocchiatti treats the play as a document of class struggle and lauds it as "a contemporary satire of the great-

est impudence." See "España y su teatro contemporáneo," *Suplemento de Insula,* No. 26 (January, 1964), p. 2.

16. Martin Esslin, *The Theater of the Absurd* (New York: Anchor, 1961), p. 90.

17. *Ibid.,* pp. 90–95, 100, and 297. The composition of *Neither Poor nor Rich* antedates by ten years the première of Ionesco's first major absurdist production, *The Bald Soprano* (1950).

18. Eduardo Haro Tecglen, *Informaciones* (Madrid, February 7, 1953), p. 7.

19. José Monleón, "La libertad de Miguel Mihura," *Miguel Mihura,* ed. José Monleón (Madrid, 1965), pp. 47–48.

20. Mihura, *Obras,* p. 721.

21. *Ibid.,* p. 120.

22. For example, the nonexistent word *pobra* is used to refer to a female pauper and *agua dura* ("hard water") is employed in the same context with *pan duro* ("hard bread").

23. Quoted in M. Sánchez Camargo, *El Alcázar* (Madrid, December 8, 1943), p. 2.

24. Emilio Clocchiatti cites this episode as evidence of the play's socio-economic intent. See *Insula,* No. 206 (January, 1964), p. 1. Juan Guerrero Zamora likewise mentions this element in his consideration of the play's philosophic implications. He views it as revealing the transition in Spain from a bourgeois society into a bureaucratic one. See his *Historia del teatro contemporáneo* (Barcelona, 1962), III, p. 175. Each of these view-points impresses us as being overstated. The socioeconomic factors in the plot are mere devices, it would seem, contributing to further the authors' satire on the ridiculous nature of a sterile language. That they function as parody is not denied, but they do not constitute the paramount focal point of the comedy.

25. See, in this connection, Adolph H. Wegener, "The Absurd in Mod-ern Literature," *Books Abroad* (Spring, 1967), pp. 150–56; also Esslin, *op. cit.,* Preface, xviii.

26. Eugène Ionesco, "The Avant-garde Theater," *World Theater,* VIII, No. 3 (Autumn, 1959), 188.

27. Laiglesia appears to have provided more moral support than actual writing. According to Ángel de las Bárcenas, Mihura contributed the basic plot and the humor, Laiglesia, the elements of mystery. See *Claridades* (Mexico, October 18, 1953), p. 22. Medardo Fraile asserts that Laiglesia's influence "is nowhere to be seen" in the play. See "Twenty Years of Theater in Spain," trans. by Mildred Boyer, *Texas Quarterly,* IV, No. 1 (Spring, 1961), 99.

28. Mihura, *Obras,* p. 40.

29. See "Autocrítica," *Marca* (Madrid, February 21, 1946), p. 4.

30. Mihura, *Obras,* p. 41.

31. See A. D. Olano, *El Alcázar* (Madrid, April 4, 1953), p. 5.

32. Quoted by Ricardo Domenech, "Reflexiones sobre la situación del teatro," *Primer Acto,* No. 42, 1963, p. 7.

33. José Monleón, "La libertad de Miguel Mihura," *Miguel Mihura,* ed. J. Monleón (Madrid, 1965), p. 55.

34. Gonzalo Torrente Ballester, "El teatro serio de un humorista," in *Miguel Mihura,* ed. J. Monleón (Madrid, 1965), p. 69.

35. For a brief summary of the play's reception in Mexico, see Eleanore M. Dial's unpublished thesis, "Critical Reaction to a Decade of Spanish Theater in Mexico, 1950-1959 (University of Missouri, 1968), pp. 96-97. Other foreign presentations or adaptations of this play have appeared in Argentina, Chile, Italy, Portugal, England, Belgium, and the United States. See Monleón, "Obras de Miguel Mihura traducidas o adaptadas a otros idiomas," *Miguel Mihura* (Madrid, 1965), p. 153. One even finds a warped adaptation of the comedy in Philadelphia's Walnut Street Theater for a short run in 1964. The play was entitled *Rich Little Rich Girl* and involved a wealthy female capitalist in a murder plot with a South American dictator. The play folded after two weeks. See Otis L. Guernsey, Jr., *The Best Plays of 1964-65* (New York: Dodd, Mead and Co., 1965), p. 371.

36. Alfredo Marqueríe, *Veinte años de teatro en España* (Madrid, 1959), p. 147.

37. Mateo Enríquez, review of "Mujer asesinadita" in *Ecclesia* (Rome, August 6, 1946).

38. *Ibid.*

39. Fernández de Asís, *Pueblo* (Madrid, February 21, 1946), p. 4.

40. Mihura's predecessor, Enrique Jardiel Poncela, accused Noel Coward of having plagiarized his own comedy, *A Round-Trip Husband* (1939), in the writing of *Blithe Spirit.* See D. R. McKay, *Enrique Jardiel Poncela* (New York: Twayne, 1974), pp. 54-55.

41. Jorge de la Cueva, *Ya* (Madrid, February 21, 1946), p. 5.

42. Alfredo Marqueríe, *ABC* (Madrid, February 21, 1946), p. 21.

43. Diez Crespo, *Arriba* (Madrid, February 21, 1946), p. 4.

44. Marqueríe, *op. cit.*

45. Theodore S. Beardsley, Jr., "The Illogical Character in Contemporary Spanish Drama," *Hispania,* XLI, No. 4 (December, 1958), p. 447.

46. A less effective English translation has been rendered as *The Case of the Woman's Nice Little Murder* by Mildred Boyer.

47. Mihura, *Obras,* p. 183.

48. *Ibid.,* p. 186.

49. *Ibid.,* p. 250.

Chapter Five

1. José Monleón, "La libertad de Miguel Mihura," *Miguel Mihura,*

ed. J. Monleón (Madrid, 1965), p. 45.

2. Ricardo Domenech, "*Tres sombreros de copa,* o Un esperpento cordial," *Ibid.,* p. 98.

3. Jorge Collar, "Los tres sombreros de copa de Miguel Mihura," *La Estafeta Literaria,* No. 164 (March 1, 1959), 17.

4. J. S., "Buenos diías, M. Labiche!", *Dimanche-Presse* (Paris, January 29, 1959).

5. The main thrust of Ionesco's observations merits repetition: "*Three Top Hats* ... has the advantage of being able to join humor to the tragic, profound truth to cleverness, which, while it is an element of caricature, reinforces and emphasizes the truth of things. The irrational style of this play can arouse the public better than formal rationalization.... Humor is the only possibility that we have of liberating ourselves from the tragicomedy of our human situation, from the insipidity of our existence. Logic is revealed in the illogic of the absurd. The work of Mihura requires a bit of effort, a certain agility of spirit on the part of the spectator, to surprise the rational through the irrational, to pass from life to dream, from dream to life. In this work the tragic is united to the comic, suffering to buffoonery, derision to gravity. It is excellent intellectual gymnastics." See Eugène Ionesco, "El humor negro contra la mixtificación," *Primer Acto,* No. 7 (March-April, 1959), pp. 63–64; see also Ionesco's prologue to *Les trois chapeaux claque,* trans. Hélène Duc and José Estrada (Paris: L'Avant-scène; Femina Théâtre, No. 191).

6. Miguel Mihura, *Obras completas* (Barcelona, 1962), p. 31.

7. Juan Emilio Aragonés, "Tres sombreros de copa," *La Estafeta Literaria,* No. 281 (December 21, 1963).

8. Monleón, *op. cit.,* p. 45.

9. Adolfo Prego, "El teatro de Miguel Mihura," *Primer Acto,* No. 10 (October, 1959), 18.

10. Personal interview with Mihura, June 9, 1967. In a later interview, however (January, 1975), Mihura stated just the opposite: "*Three Top Hats* is my best play because its language and its humor have a timeless quality that will be remembered long after I am forgotten."

11. Doris K. Arjona, "Beyond Humor: The Theater of Miguel Mihura," *Kentucky Foreign Language Quarterly,* VI, No. 2 (1959), 5. Anthony Pasquariello addresses himself to this tragicomic tone in "Miguel Mihura's *Tres sombreros de copa:* A Farce to Make You Sad," *Symposium,* XXVI, No. 1 (Spring, 1972), 57–66.

12. Francisco Sitjá, "Cincuenta años de teatro proscrito," *Insula,* No. 157 (December, 1959), 16.

13. Comment made by Enrique Llovet in "El honor en el teatro de Miguel Mihura," *Miguel Mihura,* ed. José Monleón (Madrid, 1965), p. 89.

14. Carlos Fernández Cuenca, *Teatro* (Madrid), No. 5 (March, 1933), p. 6.

15. Juan Guerrero Zamora, *Historia del teatro contemporáneo,* III (Barcelona, 1962), p. 173.

16. While many of Mihura's thieves, streetwalkers, and other lower-class individuals are often given names indicative of their profession or type, the author is not prone to tag his main characters with suggestive or ironic names. However, *Three Top Hats* is atypical in this respect. Most of the characters in the play have ironical naming, particularly Don Sacramento, the puritanical formalist, and Fany, a common prostitute. Dionisio's name is wholly ironic; he is anything but bacchic in his conduct until he meets Paula, by whom he becomes literally inebriated as well as spiritually intoxicated with the joy of unrestrained permissiveness. Paula, for her part, may be aptly named, after the Biblical Paul, for her aversion to marriage.

17. Guerrero Zamora, *op. cit.,* p. 173. One example from Don Rosario's dialogue in Scene One: "One sees the mountain, with a very fat cow on top that little by little is eating up the entire mountain" (Mihura, *Obras,* p. 48).

18. Evaristo Acevedo, *Teoría e interpretación del humor español* (Madrid, 1966), p. 248.

19. Mihura, *Obras,* p. 90.

20. *Ibid.,* p. 30.

21. *Ibid.,* p. 31.

22. Enrique Llovet, *ABC* (Madrid, September 4, 1964).

23. Quoted by Federico Carlos Sainz de Robles, *Teatro Español 1952-53* (Madrid: Aguilar, 1954), p. 92.

24. Gonzalo Torrente Ballester, "El teatro serio de un humorista," *Miguel Mihura,* ed. José Monleón (Madrid, 1965), p. 79.

25. Domenech, *op. cit.,* p. 99.

26. Mihura, *Obras,* p. 96.

27. *Ibid.,* p. 93.

28. Juan Guerrero Zamora, *op. cit.,* p. 172.

29. Torrente Ballester, *op. cit.,* p. 73.

30. Domenech, *op. cit.,* p. 99.

31. Mihura, *Obras,* pp. 68 and 94.

32. *Ibid.,* p. 71.

33. Monleón, *op. cit.,* p. 47.

34. *Ibid.,* p. 49.

35. Domenech, *op. cit.,* p. 100.

36. *Ibid.*

37. Mihura, *Obras,* p. 79.

Chapter Six

1. Mihura reports that the bellicose atmosphere in and around Rome

during 1941 and 1942 "influenced the development of the play." See his "Autocrítica," *ABC* (Madrid, February 6, 1953), 32.

2. *Ibid.*

3. José Monleón, "La libertad de Miguel Mihura," *Miguel Mihura* (Madrid, 1965), p. 56. Two other critics have been equally harsh regarding *The Stupendous Lady.* Torrente Ballester speaks of its "vacillating and indecisive character" and laments "an evident contradiction between the style of the theme and that of the dialogues." See *Arriba,* No. 6316 (Madrid, February 7, 1953), p. 12. Fernández de Asís finds "nothing worthy of mention" in the play. He calls it a work based on "a concern for evoking laughter through purely mechanical means, completely removed from humor." See *Pueblo,* No. 4178 (Madrid, February 7, 1953), p. 6.

4. *A No-Account Woman* was produced as a film in 1948. It was directed by Rafael Gil and starred María Félix and Antonio Vilar in the principal roles.

5. Luis Molera Manglano, Review in *La Estafeta Literaria,* No. 179 (October 15, 1959), p. 14.

6. Since 1963 *Carlota* has also enjoyed success as a detective thriller in American college classrooms. See Edith B. Sublette's edition (New York: Odyssey, 1963).

7. Arcadio Baquero, *El Alcázar* (Madrid, April 13, 1957), p. 24.

8. Ruth Richardson, "Algunos datos sobre dramaturgos españoles contemporáneos," *Revista Hispánica Moderna,* 34 (1968), p. 420.

9. See Elías Gómez Picazo, *Madrid* (November 21, 1958), p. 10; V. Fernández Asís, *Pueblo* (Madrid, November 21, 1958), p. 14; and Molero Manglano, *La Estafeta Literaria,* No. 157 (December 6, 1958), p. 10.

10. Manuel Adrio, *ABC* (Madrid, February 6, 1965), p. 75.

11. Arcadio Baquero, *El Alcázar* (Madrid, February 6, 1965), p. 29.

12. García Pavón, *Arriba* (Madrid, March 4, 1965), p. 16.

13. See, for instance, Alfredo Marquíe, *Pueblo* (Madrid, March 4, 1965), p. 22; Valencia, *Marca* (Madrid, March 6, 1965), p. 11; and Nicolás González Ruiz, *Ya* (Madrid, March 4, 1965).

14. Mihura's portrait of Julieta is reminiscent of Carlos Arniches' treatment of the provincial Florita in *Miss Trevélez.*

15. Juan Emilio Aragonés, "'El punto de apoyo' de Miguel Mihura," *La Estafeta Literaria,* No. 313 (March 13, 1965), p. 9.

16. S. Samuel Trifilo, "The Madrid Theater: 1967–68," *Hispania,* LII, No. 4 (December, 1969), p. 913.

17. José María de Quinto, *Insula,* No. 221 (April, 1965), p. 15.

Chapter Seven

1. This reconciliation with standard morality through marriage is an ending imposed on the play by Spanish censorship. It is interesting to

observe that in the Mexican version of *Three in Dim Light,* directed by Julián Soler at the Teatro Arena (October, 1954–February, 1955), this accommodating epilogue in which the reformed protagonist marries his servant girl was dropped. See *Revista Mexicana de Cultura,* No. 398 (Mexico, November 14, 1954), p. 13; and *Claridades* (Mexico, October 31, 1954), p. 20.

2. See V. Fernández Asís, *Pueblo* (Madrid, November 26, 1953), p. 13.

3. Rafael Vásquez Zamora, *Insula,* No. 102 (April, 1954), p. 12.

4. V. Fernández Asís, *Pueblo* (Madrid, April 19, 1954), p. 6.

5. See Gonzalo Torrente Ballester, *Arriba* (Madrid, April 18, 1954), p. 18; and Adolfo Prego, *Informaciones* (Madrid, April 19, 1954), p. 6.

6. Nicolás González Ruiz, *Ya* (Madrid, April 18, 1954), p. 7. This is the same position held by critics favorably disposed to the audacious currents of humor found in the theater of Mihura's predecessor, Enrique Jardiel Poncela.

7. The emergence of social and individual emancipation is poignantly reflected in Jardiel's comedies, *A Sleepless Spring Night* (1927) and *The Weaker Sex Has Undergone Gymnastics* (1946). For an intelligent review of Martínez Sierra's feminist plays see Patricia W. O'Connor, "A Spanish Precursor to Women's Lib: The Heroine in Gregorio Martínez Sierra's Theater," *Hispania,* LV, No. 4 (December, 1974), pp. 865–72.

8. In a few plays, most notably *My Beloved Juan,* Mihura endows some secondary female characters with independence, but his protagonists generally function within the framework of a male-dominated society. This subject is treated with perceptive and scholarly care by Marilynn I. Ward, "Themes of Submission, Dominance, Independence and Romantic Love: The Female Figure in the Post-"Avant-Garde" Plays of Miguel Mihura, Unpublished doctoral thesis (University of Colorado, 1974).

9. See Juan Guerrero Zamora, *El Alcázar* (Madrid, April 11, 1955), p. 8.

10. Professor Cyrus C. DeCoster takes a similar view in his summary of the play's unstated aim: "... under the guise of criticizing the mores of another age, the author satirizes various aspects of the character and customs of his fellow countrymen, the working habits, courtship, the position of women, and the difficult economic situation of the middle classes." See "The Theatrical Season in Madrid 1954–55," *Hispania,* XXXIX, No. 2 (May, 1956), p. 184.

11. Marion P. Holt, *The Contemporary Spanish Theater (1949–1972),* (Boston, 1975), p. 56.

12. Alfredo Marquerie, *ABC* (Madrid, April 10, 1955), p. 40.

13. It has been said that the Spanish woman of 1900, a product of rigid social conventions, could aspire to become either a queen, a teacher, a telephone operator, or a tobacco shop proprietor.

14. V. Fernández Asís, *Pueblo* (Madrid, April 11, 1955), p. 8.

15. Remarks conveyed in a personal interview, January, 1975.

16. *Ibid.*

17. See Juan Gerrero Zamora, *El Alcázar* (Madrid, December 2, 1955), p. 8; V. Fernández Asís, *Pueblo* (Madrid, December 2, 1955), p. 13; and Torrente Ballester, *Arriba* (Madrid, December 2, 1955), p. 18.

18. Alfredo Marqueríe, *ABC* (Madrid,December 2, 1955), p. 43.

19. Valencia and Torrente go one step further in their respective negative reviews, stating that Mihura's dialogue is so exclusive and absorbing that "it constitutes the core of the play's existence," and consequently "debilitates or reduces to almost nothing" the remaining elements of the comedy. See Valencia, *Marca* (Madrid, November 24, 1961), p. 13; and Torrente, *Arriba* (Madrid, November 25, 1961), p. 18.

20. Alfredo Marqueríe, *ABC* (Madrid, November 24, 1961), p. 75.

Chapter Eight

1. Marion P. Holt, *The Contemporary Spanish Theater (1949-1972)* (Boston, 1975), p. 57.

2. This idea is fostered in the Introduction to *Mi adorado Juan,* ed. by John V. Falconieri and Anthony M. Pasquariello (New York, 1964), p. xii.

3. In general V. Fernández Asís, Juan Guerrero Zamora, and Torrente Ballester accused Mihura of compromising his talents to satisfy the public's taste for happy endings and sugary-sweet resolutions. See their respective reviews of *Mi adorado Juan* in the Madrid dailies, *Pueblo,* p. 11; *El Alcázar,* p.8; and *Arriba,* p. 15, all dated January 12, 1956.

4. Pedro Laín Entralgo believes that Maribel's three companions exemplify the vein of Cervantine humor running through Mihura's plays. He sees Rufi, Pili, and Nini cast from the same mold as Cariharta, Gananciosa, and Escalanta of Miguel Cervantes' novel, *Rinconete y Cortadillo.* See *Tras el amor y la risa* (Barcelona: Delos-Aymá, 1967), p. 162.

5. Manuel María, "Miguel Mihura: la fama, el dinero y la crisis," *Madrid* (December 13, 1966), p. 7.

6. Ángel Laborda, "Entrevista," *Informaciones* (Madrid, September 29, 1959), p. 8.

7. Gonzalo Torrente Ballester, *Arriba* (Madrid, September 30, 1959), p. 20.

8. Valencia, *Marca* (Madrid, September 30, 1959), p. 9.

9. Holt, *op. cit.,* p. 61.

10. Alfredo Marqueríe, *Pueblo* (Madrid, October 26, 1963), p. 29.

11. The alleged social criticism of Spain in this play has been greatly overstated by critics and readers who see in the clash between Andrés, son of a traditional Nationalist, and Don Pedro, the anarchistic Asturian Republican, the first clear demonstration of political conscience in

Mihura's theater. We tend to see in this, however, a convenient thematic device for sharpening the comical contrast between the two characters. Neither *Ninette* play is committed to a treatment of the tragic problems of Spanish exiles and emigrants. If the enigma of the "Two Spains" emerges, it is merely incidental to the farcical, humorous manner in which Mihura depicts the expatriated Pedro.

Chapter Nine

1. Alfredo Marqueríe, "A Centenary of Spanish Theatre," *Topic: A Journal of the Liberal Arts,* No. 15 (Spring, 1968), p. 31.

Selected Bibliography

PRIMARY SOURCES

(Since not all contemporary plays appear in print, some indication of availability is opportune.)

La bella Dorotea, in *Teatro Hispánico,* ed. Mary Jackson and Edenia Guillermo (Skokie, Illinois: National Textbook Co., 1973), pages 89–170.
Carlota, ed. Edith B. Sublette (New York: Odyssey, 1963).
"Colección teatro," Ediciones Alfil (Madrid: Editorial Escelicer). Twenty-one of Mihura's plays have been published in this inexpensive series: Nos. 41, 51, 61, 68, 92, 112, 116, 128, 149, 210, 233, 252, 334, 369, 415, 462, 479, 484, 542, 611, and 622.
Maribel y la extraña familia, ed. Anthony V. Cervone (Orlando, Florida: Florida Technological University, 1972).
Melocotón en almíbar and *Ninette y un señor de Murcia,* "Colección Austral" #1570 (Madrid: Espasa Calpe, 1974).
Mi adorado Juan, ed. J.V. Falconieri and A.M. Pasquariello (New York: Blaisdell Publishing Co., 1964).
Obras completas (Barcelona: Editorial AHR, 1962). Includes prologue by Edgar Neville, Mihura's "Introducción a Tres sombreros de copa", the complete text of thirteen plays, and three prose writings entitled "Viaje a la feria de Sevilla," "Sentado alegre en la popa," and "Mis memorias."
El seductor (Pequeña alta comedia en un acto). Special supplement, *La Estafeta Literaria* (Madrid, 1965). Premiered May 26, 1965 in Madrid's Teatro Comedia to celebrate the 500th performance of *Ninette y un señor de Murcia.*
Teatro Español, ed. Federico Carlos Sainz de Robles (Madrid: Aguilar). Contains ten of Mihura's plays with selected reviews and theatrical documentations in volumes for 1952–53, 1953–54, 1954–55, 1955–56, 1956–57, 1959–60, 1963–64, 1964–65, 1966–67, and 1967–68.
Teatro selecto (Madrid: Escelicer, 1967). Includes: *Tres sombreros de copa, A media luz los tres, Melocotón en almíbar, Maribel y la extraña familia, Sublime decisión,* and *Ninette y un señor de Murcia.*
Tres sombreros de copa, La bella Dorotea, Ninette y un señor de Murcia, in *Miguel Mihura,* ed. José Monleón (Madrid: Taurus Ediciones, 1965).

145

Tres sombreros de copa and *Maribel y la extraña familia,*"Colección Austral" #1537 (Madrid: Espasa Calpe, 1973).
¡Viva lo imposible! o El contable de estrellas (Madrid: Edition of the co-authors Miguel Mihura and Joaquín Calvo-Sotelo, 1951).

Plays and Dates of Their Premières

Long Live the Impossible, or The Star Accountant (*¡Viva lo imposible! o El contable de estrellas*) (Collaboration with Joaquín Calvo-Sotelo)	November 24, 1939
Neither Poor nor Rich but the Exact Reverse (*Ni pobre ni rico, sino todo lo contrario*) (Collaboration with Tono)	December 17, 1943
The Case of the Slightly Murdered Woman (*El caso de la mujer asesinadita*) (Collaboration with Álvaro de Laiglesia)	February 20, 1946
Three Top Hats (*Tres sombreros de copa*)	November 24, 1952
The Case of the Stupendous Lady (*El caso de la señora estupenda*)	February 6, 1953
A No-Account Woman (*Una mujer cualquiera*)	April 4, 1953
Three in Dim Light (*A media luz los tres*)	November 25, 1953
The Case of the Gentleman Dressed in Violet (*El caso del señor vestido de violeta*)	April 17, 1954
Sublime Decision (*Sublime decisión*)	April 9, 1955
Canasta (*La canasta*) (Unpublished)	December 1, 1955
My Beloved Juan (*Mi adorado Juan*)	January 11, 1956
Carlota	April 12, 1957
Peaches and Syrup (*Melocotón en almíbar*)	November 20, 1958
Maribel and the Strange Family (*Maribel y la extraña familia*)	September 29, 1959
Madame Renard's Chalet (*El chalet de Madame Renard*)	November 23, 1961
Ladies of the Night (*Las entretenidas*)	September 12, 1962
Lovely Dorotea (*La bella Dorotea*)	October 25, 1963
Ninette and a Gentleman from Murcia (*Ninette y un señor de Murcia*)	September 3, 1964
Miracle at the López House (*Milagro en casa de los López*)	September 24, 1964 (Barcelona) February 5, 1965 (Madrid)

The Teapot (La tetera)	March 15, 1965
Ninette, Paris Fashions (Ninette, modas de París)	September 7, 1966
The Decent Woman (La decente)	September 4, 1967
Only Love and the Moon Bring Good Fortune	September 12, 1968
(Sólo el amor y la luna traen fortuna)	

Other Primary Writings

La Ametralladora (Salamanca, Valladolid, Bilbao, Santander, 1936–1939). The years posted represent the journal's livelihood as a business venture. The first actual issue is dated January 18, 1937; the final number, June 26, 1938.

La Codorniz (Madrid, 1941–1944). Mihura's tenure as director began with the first issue, dated June 8, 1941, and terminated with issue number 147, dated March 26, 1944.

Mis Memorias (Barcelona: Taurus Ediciones, 1948). A miscellany of quasi-autobiographical reminiscences spanning his boyhood, youth, and early career through the management of *La Codorniz.*

SECONDARY SOURCES

The titles of articles and reviews not appearing here may be obtained by consulting the bibliography sections in the doctoral theses by McKay and Ward, listed below.

1. In English

ARJONA, DORIS K. "Beyond Humor: The Theater of Miguel Mihura," *Kentucky Foreign Language Quarterly* VI, No. 2 (1959), 63–68. Readable insights into the absurdity and humanity of Mihura's humor.

BORING, PHYLLIS Z. "The Bases of Humor in the Contemporary Spanish Theatre," (Doctoral thesis, University of Florida, 1965). Lucid study defining the humor of situation in eleven of Mihura's plays. Portions have been published in *Kentucky Foreign Language Quarterly* XIII (1966), 41–51; *Modern Drama* II,i (May 1967), 82–86; and *Romance Notes* IX (1968), 201–05.

DAVISON, DARLYN D. "The Role of the Women in Miguel Mihura's Plays," (Doctoral thesis, Florida State University, 1974). Lively approach to the behavior and interaction of the playwright's decisive females in twenty-one plays.

HOLT, MARION P. *The Contemporary Spanish Theater (1949–1972).* (Boston: Twayne, 1975). Recommended introduction to an important period of Spanish dramatic literature. Positive assessment of Mihura's contributions on pages 51–67.

McKay, Douglas R. "The Avant-Garde Theater of Miguel Mihura," (Doctoral thesis, Michigan State University, 1968). Life and early career; analysis with respect to theme, structure, characterization, and dramatic content of the four plays Mihura wrote before 1950.

Morales, Maria Victoria. "The Farcical Mode in the Spanish Theater of the Twentieth Century" (Doctoral thesis, Columbia University, 1969). Occasional references to importance of Mihura's theater.

Ward, Marilynn I. "Themes of Submission, Dominance, Independence and Romantic Love: The Female Figure in the Post-"Avant-Garde" Plays of Miguel Mihura," (Doctoral thesis, University of Colorado, 1974). Highly recommended study on the role of women in eighteen of Mihura's plays. Excellent bibliography.

2. In Spanish

Acevedo, Evaristo. Teoría e interpretación del humor español. Colección "Crítica de las artes," (Madrid: Editora Nacional, 1966). Pages 107–10 and 247–56 present a schematic and unfavorable evaluation of Mihura and his work on La Codorniz.

————. Treinta años de risa: 1940–1970. (Madrid: Editorial Magisterio Español, 1973). Deals sporadically with Mihura's management of and contributions to La Codorniz.

Aragonés, Juan Emilio. Teatro español de posguerra. (Madrid: Publicaciones Españolas, 1971). Pages 14–19 deal expressly with Mihura's theater; a concise summary on the value of his best plays.

Álvaro, Francisco. El espectador y la crítica (Valladolid: Author's edition, yearly publication). An annual compendium since 1958 featuring theater facts and critical commentaries abstracted from reviews.

Cabello, George T. "El humor en el teatro de Miguel Mihura," (Doctoral thesis, University of Arizona, 1974). Useful introduction to Mihura's theater.

Carballo, J. Rof. et al., El teatro de humor en España (Madrid: Editora Nacional, 1966). Highly recommended essays on major dramatists of Mihura's generation, including Calvo-Sotelo, Jardiel Poncela, and Tono. Pages 201–30 deal specifically with Miguel Mihura.

Crescioni Neggers, Gladys. "Miguel Mihura: Iniciador del teatro del absurdo," La Estafeta Literaria, No. 572 (Madrid, September 15, 1975), 9–11. Mihura's personal reflections on his career and the nature of his dramatic humor.

Galán, Diego. ¿Reírse en España? (El humor español en el banquillo). (Valencia: Fernando Torres Editor, 1974). Occasional observations on the importance and the impact of La Codorniz.

García Lorente, Juana María. "El humor y los recursos cómicos en el teatro de Miguel Mihura," (Doctoral thesis, University of Barcelona, 1973). Somewhat diffuse study of Mihura's comic inventiveness.

GUERRERO ZAMORA, JUAN. *Historia del teatro contemporáneo,* Vol. III (Barcelona: Juan Flors, 1962). Pages 171–78 provide an informative scholarly review of Mihura's avant-garde plays.

LAÍN ENTRALGO, PEDRO. *La aventura de leer* (Madrid: Espasa Calpe-Austral, 1946). Pages 120–33 deal perceptively with the humor of *La Codorniz* under Mihura's editorship.

LARA, FERNANDO and DIEGO GALÁN. "Miguel Mihura, burgués con espíritu de 'clochard'," *Triunfo,* No. 500 (April 29, 1972), 40–43. Lively interview. Mihura speaks of his weariness, retirement, age, health, and disillusionment.

MARQUERÍE, ALFREDO. *Veinte años de teatro en España.* (Madrid: Editora Nacional, 1959). Madrid theater scene from 1939 to 1959. Cursory glimpse at Mihura's theater on pages 145–53.

MONLEÓN, JOSÉ (Ed.). *Miguel Mihura* (Madrid: Taurus Ediciones, 1965). Valuable collection of bibliographical data, critical essays, and miscellaneous observations, with complete text of *Tres sombreros de copa, La bella Dorotea,* and *Ninette y un señor de Murcia.*

—————. *Treinta años de teatro de la derecha.* (Barcelona: Tusquets Editor, 1971). Several provocative chapters discuss Mihura's hits and misses. See especially Chapter Four for a discerning comparison between Mihura and Jardiel Poncela.

PÉREZ COBAS, PATRICIO. *El teatro de Miguel Mihura.* (Doctoral thesis, University of Madrid, 1965). Inordinately prolix, void of critical substance despite its 200+ pages.

PONCE, FERNANDO. *Miguel Mihura* (Madrid: EPESA, 1972). An insubstantial, wearisome, rambling monograph of questionable value.

PREGO, ADOLFO. "El teatro de Miguel Mihura," *Primer Acto,* No. 10. (October 1959), 17–19. Endorses Mihura's bourgeois theater for its power of language and characterizations.

RUIZ RAMÓN, FRANCISCO. *Historia del teatro español.* Vol. 2. (Madrid: Alianza Editorial, 1971). Excellent overview by an accomplished scholar. Chapter Six (pp. 358–75) treats Mihura's post-war theater with incisive clarity.

VALENCIA, ANTONIO. "El teatro de Miguel Mihura," *España, hoy,* No. 7 (1970), 27–32. Considers Mihura's work in three stages: the absurd, theater of intrigue, and memorable character studies.

WOFSY, SAMUEL A. "La calidad literaria del teatro de Miguel Mihura," *Hispania* XLIII, No. 2 (May 1960), 214–18. A breezy vindication of Mihura's artistry.

YOUNG, RAYMOND A. "Sombre el humorismo de Miguel Mihura," *Quaderni Ibero-Americani* 37 (1969), 30–36; also in *Hispanófila* 36 (May, 1969), 21–29. Deals scantily with six comedies.

3. In Norwegian

MUUR, INGEBORG. "Miguel Mihura's Teater." (Oslo, 1966). A very general, ambitious approach to humor, themes, and characterization in Mihura's plays.

Index

(Mihura's works and writings of collaboration are listed under his name)